# SUPERVISION AND STAFF DEVELOPMENT IN THE BLOCK

Sally J. Zepeda
R. Stewart Mayers

EYE ON EDUCATION
6 DEPOT WAY WEST, SUITE 106
LARCHMONT, NY 10538
(914) 833–0551
(914) 833–0761 fax

**Library of Congress Cataloging-in-Publication Data**

Zepeda, Sally J. 1956–
  Supervision and staff development in the block / by Sally J. Zepeda and R. Stewart Mayers.
      p.   cm.
  Includes bibliographical references and index.
  ISBN 1-883001-83-8
    1. Block scheduling (Education)—Planning. 2. School supervision—Planning. 3. Teachers—In-service training.   I. Mayers, R. Stewart. 1959– . II. Title.
LB 3032.2.Z46    2000
370'.71'55—dc21                                                                9941000
                                                                                  CIP


10 9 8 7 6 5 4 3 2 1

Editorial and production services provided by
Richard H. Adin Freelance Editorial Services
52 Oakwood Blvd., Poughkeepsie, NY 12603-4112
(914-471-3566)

# *Also Available from* EYE ON EDUCATION

# ABOUT THE AUTHORS

Dr. Sally J. Zepeda has served as a high school teacher, director of special programs, assistant principal, and principal at the elementary, middle, and high school levels. Sally is an assistant professor at the University of Georgia in the Department of Educational Leadership, where she teaches instructional supervision and other courses dealing with professional development. She is widely published in the areas of educational administration, supervision of teaching, and leadership. Her books include *Hands-on Leadership Tools for Principals* (with Raymond Calabrese and Gary Short); *The Reflective Supervisor: A Practical Guide for Educators* (with Raymond Calabrese); *Special Programs in Regular Schools: Historical Foundations, Standards, and Contemporary Issues* (with Michael Langenbach); and *Staff Development: Practices that Promote Leadership in Learning Communities*.

Dr. Zepeda is the Book and Audio Review editor for the *Journal of Staff Development*, and is the editor of the American Educational Research Association's *Supervision SIG Newsletter*. She is a member of the Council of Professors of Instructional Supervision (COPIS), serves as a reviewer for several scholarly journals, and is on the Editorial Board of the *Journal of Curriculum and Supervision*. She is a lifetime Fellow in the Foundation for Excellence in Teaching.

R. Stewart Mayers, a former classroom teacher and department chair, has taught mathematics (middle school through advanced placement calculus), history, and German in both traditional and block schedules. As department chair, he adapted a mathematics curriculum for the transition from a six-period day to an accelerated block. Stewart is currently pursuing his doctorate at the University of Georgia where he is also a graduate assistant in the Department of Educational Leadership.

# TABLE OF CONTENTS

# Dedication

To Sally Riley who nurtured many teachers in the block at Norman High School (Norman, Oklahoma). Although Sally retired as a career assistant principal in 1998, her legacy continues through the lives she touched with enduring support for the efforts of teachers.

*SJZ*

To my parents, Robert and Doris Mayers, for always believing in me, and to my wife, Mary Ellen, for being my best friend.

*RSM*

# Acknowledgments

There are always numerous people who assist authors writing a book. We are grateful to the many teachers and administrators who shared their insights about block scheduling.

We are indebted to our reviewers, Professor Nan Restine, Oklahoma State University, and Principal John M. Brucato, Milford High School (Massachusetts), for their insights. Our book is stronger as a result of their willingness to spend time making suggestions and sharing their expertise.

Finally, we are indebted to Bob Sickles for his unyielding enthusiasm, support, and dedication to producing books of high quality.

*SJZ*
*RSM*

Please send all correspondence regarding this book to:
Eye On Education
6 Depot Way West #106
Larchmont, NY 10538

# LIST OF FIGURES

# INTRODUCTION

*Supervision and Staff Development in the Block* is offered as a resource for administrators and teachers who continually seek to grow professionally. The two connecting themes throughout this book are the intertwined nature of supervision and staff development and how these processes can empower teachers as professional learners. Effective supervision and staff development are impossible to separate; they share the same principal objectives (e.g., improvement of instruction and facilitation of teachers' lifelong learning). Moreover, supervision and staff development have many common attributes (e.g., short- and long-term goal setting, dialogue, reflection, and feedback).

In this book, we strike a balance between research and practical applications. It is our hope that, while grounded in the latest thought and scant available research, this book might be a practical, accessible tool for administrators and teachers involved in all phases of implementing and maintaining momentum for growth in schools that have or are considering adopting a block schedule.

In Chapter 1, reflection, inquiry, self-analysis, and dialogue are recast to fit the linkages between supervisory and staff development models. The Coherence Model is introduced as a blueprint for unifying supervision and staff development. Also explored are the organizational structures that need to be examined if the transition to the block is to promote learning. The tasks that need schoolwide focus to facilitate a smooth transition to the block are explored with an emphasis in building both organizational and professional capacity. In Chapter 2, the most frequently utilized block schedules (e.g., accelerated block, alternating block, and Copernican) are explored along with the advantages and disadvantages of each. The ways in which teaching and learning change within the context of the block schedule is presented against the backdrop of brain research and Gardner's Multiple Intelligence Theory.

Chapter 3 discusses new roles for assistant principals, department chairs, instructional deans, and lead teachers. The reader is led through the process of developing a profile of the administrative team in order to identify strengths while examining the organizational structure and program in place to support professional development. This chapter concludes with a discussion of how principals can formulate the vision necessary to maximize learning in the block schedule.

Staff development initiatives that help ready teachers for effective instruction in the block are presented in Chapter 4. Auditing strategies (e.g., curriculum mapping and pacing) along with teaching strategies that enhance learning in block periods are explored, including descriptions of hands-on instructional simulations. This chapter culminates with a sample comprehensive staff development plan for schools that are preparing to implement a block schedule. Chapter 5 shifts to how and why instructional supervision needs to change to reflect the complexities of teaching in the block. Instruments suitable for formal supervision in the block are offered, followed by a discussion of techniques of informal supervision and their utilization in the block classroom. Finally, new twists in the application of such processes as action research, auditing, coaching, and videotape analysis of teaching are presented as differentiated forms of supervision.

Staff development and supervision that assists teachers in maintaining the momentum for the block are presented in Chapter 6. The underpinnings of job-embedded learning provide principals, teachers, and staff developers with the tools necessary to make adult learning more relevant to a block schedule. Several master scheduling models are presented in order for principals to find time for their teachers to learn.

Chapter 7, written by Judith A. Ponticell and Arturo Olivarez, details concrete approaches for evaluating the impact of the block schedule. Through program evaluation, the organization will be able to determine what types of staff development and supervision are necessary to keep the block moving. The types of evaluation are examined in such a way that the principal and other stakeholders will be able to make informed decisions about developing program evaluation that can detail results. The chapter leads the reader through making several decisions: what type of evaluation to conduct; how to frame an evaluation; how to determine if an outside evaluator is needed; what types of information (data) can give what results; and how to frame an evaluation report for a variety of audiences.

We hope that principals and teachers will feel a sense of comfort and confidence in making the commitment for learning in the block while reading this book.

*Sally J. Zepeda*
*R. Stewart Mayers*

# 1

# LINKING SUPERVISION AND STAFF DEVELOPMENT: PREPARING SCHOOLS FOR THE BLOCK

## CHAPTER OBJECTIVES

- ◆ Describe ways in which principals can help to ready teachers for the block.
- ◆ Identify processes and applications that link supervision and staff development.
- ◆ Discuss the conditions needed to foster more collaborative, professional interactions.
- ◆ Highlight structures that need careful attention while moving into a block schedule.

The changes associated with moving a high school or a middle school with a traditional *master* schedule to a *block* are immense. The entire workday, as many teachers have known it, looks different. Comfortable routines change: class period length, the number of passing periods, and the pattern of teacher planning time. Instructional and classroom routines also change; moreover, these changes send a signal that teachers have different learning needs. Only more expansive and *correct* types of supervision and staff development that are inextricably linked can meet these needs. Strategies to help meet the growing pains associated with changes in practices (instructional, staff development, and supervision) are addressed in subsequent chapters.

The supervisory and staff development practices presented in these chapters will be moot, however, unless changes are made in the very structure of the organization. Structural changes are not achieved through superficial window dressing. The capability of the school to grow rests in the ability of the principal to build organizational capacity and to align the efforts of the organization with its people. To achieve alignment, the existing organizational structures and patterns, or those under construction, require a type of purposeful monitoring. Through the process of monitoring, the needs of the organization and its people will surface. Supervisory efforts to monitor and to plan for shifts can prevent shock waves from engulfing time and hindering the efforts of teachers from focusing on their learning needs.

## SHARING LEADERSHIP: GETTING READY FOR CHANGE

A major tenet of supervision and staff development is *change*. Informed principals recognize that purposeful change does not occur easily or naturally. For the implementation of a block schedule to be successful, schools must recognize that change needs to be systemic if the initiative is to be enduring. Fullan (1993) believes that "Teachers as change agents are the *sine qua non* of getting anywhere" (p. 6). For the restructuring of a school to be successful, teachers must be integrally involved. Moving to a block schedule needs more than the commitment of the principal. Ownership of change takes place only when teachers assume a leadership role in the decision-making, planning, and implementation of change. Sarason (1992) believes that:

> ...There must be change in the power structure. Teachers must be an integral part of...decision making if changes are to be truly effective, since it is up to the teachers to be the main implementers of change in our schools. (p. 4)

The teachers are the ones in the trenches. If the teachers do not embrace the block, the new schedule will merely be a surface change with little lasting impact.

Effective principals engage teachers in solving the sometimes thorny problems of instruction by creating opportunities for teachers to examine their own practices. By creating a momentum for change, the principal, "Motivate[s] all employees to work to their fullest potential" (Pasternack & Viscio, 1998, p. 67).

## READINESS FOR CHANGE:
## THE NORM OF SHARED DECISION MAKING

Perhaps the most often neglected step in any staff development initiative is the readiness stage. Both the organization and its people need time to get ready for a block schedule. Critical decision making occurs during the readiness stage: developing and focusing the vision, setting goals, and selecting programs and practices to bring these goals to fruition (Wood, Killian, McQuarrie, & Thompson, 1993). Before an organization can undergo a restructuring effort (e.g., implementing a block schedule), principals need to empower teachers to make critical decisions beyond their classrooms. Traditionally, decision making is a function of the principal. Without active, meaningful involvement and a spirit of collaboration, those furthest from the levels of implementation will continue to make decisions.

In a recent study, Shen (1998) compares principals' versus teachers' perceptions of teacher influence in making schoolwide decisions. The study finds that principals believe teachers' influence in schoolwide decision making is substantial; however, teachers believe that their sphere of influence is still limited to the classroom. This conclusion supports findings of an earlier study that showed that most principals perceived little need for teachers to have input in many schoolwide decisions (Lucas, Brown, and Markus, 1991).

Lucas et al. (1991) also concluded that principals of larger schools were less likely to involve teachers in decision making than their counterparts from smaller schools. In addition, principals believe decisions concerning major expenditures of resources are least likely to require teacher involvement. Regardless of school size, all principals face the tension of empowering teachers while simultaneously attempting to satisfy mandates from the central office. Sarason (1997) describes this tension:

> The principal sees [his/her] role as "in between" the needs and problems of students and teachers, on the one hand, and policies, pressures, and attitudes of those in higher positions, on the other hand....This job prepares you to be a tightrope walker in the circus, except...[you] don't...have a safety net. (p. 85)

Admittedly, this *tightrope* effect can deter principals' efforts at involving teachers in making schoolwide decisions. Klecker and Loadman (1998) state that the "...move from sole decision maker in control of everything to being an instructional leader...is a very large one" (p. 368). However, empowered teachers, actively involved in decision making, are "A key dimension...to achieve positive and lasting change" (Klecker & Loadman, 1998, p. 367).

In a 1994 study, Blase and Blase identify eight behaviors that principals use to successfully empower teachers:

- Modeling, building, and persistently supporting an environment of trust among teachers, whom they consider professionals and experts;
- Systematically structuring the school to encourage authentic collaboration by establishing readiness and common goals and by responding to the school's unique characteristics;
- Supporting shared governance efforts by providing professional development and basic resources;

- Supporting teacher experimentation and innovation, granting professional autonomy, and viewing failure as an opportunity to learn;
- Modeling professional behavior, especially by exhibiting caring, optimism, honesty, friendliness, and enthusiasm;
- Encouraging risk taking and minimizing threat (or constraints on teacher freedom and growth);
- Praising teachers and using other symbolic rewards (e.g., valuing and respecting teachers); and,
- Setting the stage for discussing and solving the metaproblems of a school through effective communication, openness and trust; the use of action research, group participation in decision making; and the use of effective procedural methods for solving problems. (p. 127)

The ability of principals and teachers to interact as professionals on an equal playing field is critical in readying for change.

## TEACHER READINESS FOR CHANGE

Gordon (1999) identifies five levels of organizational readiness:

- Cultural Readiness: commitment to change is possible because of high trust level, open communication, and collegiality;
- Conceptual Readiness: a common vision is developed;
- Personal Readiness: concerns of individual stakeholders have been addressed;
- Political Readiness: support is secured from the central office and community; and
- Resource Readiness: necessary resources for the initiative are acquired. (pp. 48–53)

To understand Gordon's levels of readiness, it is important to note that these levels encompass a macro-organizational perspective, but can also be relevant in readying individuals for change. Regardless of the nature of the change, both the efforts of the organization and its people need to be aligned. Without this alignment, little lasting impact will be realized for the organization or its people. Alignment ensures unity of purpose.

*Cultural readiness* for teachers begins with empowerment. Without involvement in the decision-making process, teacher commitment to change is difficult. Teachers, who are often disenfranchised, can feel devalued and find trusting other stakeholders difficult. Trust needs to be developed *within* the teaching faculty as well as *between* teachers and other stakeholders (e.g., parents, staff, and administrators). Communication needs to be reciprocal. Teachers need to know that their point of view is important and valued. Blase and Blase (1998) believe that "...Professional interaction is key to empowerment..." (p. 12).

From a *conceptual readiness* perspective, participation in the decision-making process assists teachers in assuming ownership of change. Ownership of an initiative motivates teacher involvement in constructing a shared vision with the school community. This is the foundation of conceptual readiness for change. From this vision, the broad goals of a new initiative are formed.

A final level of readiness for teachers is *resource readiness*. For teachers to be adequately prepared to implement a new initiative, they must be properly equipped with the resources (e.g., release time, teaching materials, and time for critical dialogue and reflection). The principal will need to secure funding, enlist the support of the central office, and have the latitude to manipulate time and other resources needed to move to a block.

## PROCESSES AND APPLICATIONS THAT LINK SUPERVISION AND STAFF DEVELOPMENT

Although there are differences, *effective* supervision and staff development share many of the same processes. Short- and long-term goal setting, dialogue, feedback, reflection, and analysis of practices are inherent in both. Building-level administrators might conduct supervision, or peers might coach each other utilizing supervisory processes such as the pre-observation conference, the observation, and the post-observation conference (baseline processes of all supervisory models). Commonalties that foster professional growth are:

- Short- and long-term goal setting;
- Dialogue, reflection, and self-analysis;
- Feedback; and,
- Multiple opportunities for the refinement of instructional practice.

## SHORT- AND LONG-TERM GOAL SETTING

Goal setting is a critical component of professional growth and can assist in linking both supervision and staff development. Setting individual goals helps to establish the supervisory relationship and to plan for staff development activities. It also serves as a beginning point in assessing overall performance and growth at the end of the year (e.g., Acheson & Gall, 1997).

Goal-setting conferences are conducted for two reasons:

- Working with teachers to develop goals (both long- and short-term) can assist in establishing a professional relationship between teachers and administrators; and,
- Goal-setting conferences, held at the beginning of the year, can help teachers target areas that they are interested in pursuing through staff development, supervision, independent study, or formal coursework.

The process is enhanced if the format for setting goals includes those that center on:

- Instruction;
- Classroom procedures;
- Student achievement (e.g., how teachers are going to measure the impact of their instruction on gains in student learning); and,
- Professional development (e.g., starting a masters degree or attending a cooperative learning seminar).

Figure 1.1 depicts a sample goal-setting form.

## FIGURE 1.1. SAMPLE GOAL-SETTING FORM

### High School USA

Name: _____    Grade Level: _____

Department: _____    Courses Taught: _____

Please take time to reflect on your professional learning priorities for the year and develop one or two goals for each area. We'll meet in the next week or two to discuss your goals. My role is to learn what's important to you and to discover ways in which I can be of assistance to you in meeting your goals. I look forward to meeting with you.

Instructional Goal (s):

Classroom Procedure Goal (s):

Student Achievement Goal (s):

Professional Development Goal (s):

Date: _____

Encouraging teachers to focus on both short-and long-term goals can assist them in staying focused on their development, and can assist the principal in providing the necessary support for teachers. Goal setting is ineffective, however, if there is no follow-through. Individual goal setting can also boost organizational development and growth. If the principal tracks instructional goals, then the principal can begin to profile the needs and aspirations of teachers across grade levels and subject areas. For example, if the freshman English teachers are interested in exploring the topic of reader response, then the principal can concentrate on providing staff development opportunities that are more relevant to that need. The principal is also able to coordinate the most cost-effective measures in finding materials such as journals, books, videos, and local experts (from both within the building and outside it) to focus efforts.

Tracking learning needs can be efficiently achieved by using a spreadsheet or data base program to help sort faculty by grade level, subject area, and by interest. Figure 1.2 provides a sample spreadsheet printout for tracking goals.

An organizational function that can be enhanced by personal goal setting is charting the course of the school itself. Effective schools have a plan for the present and the future. Hopefully, there is a relationship between the goals of the school and the professional goals of its teachers. With alignment of goals, can come a convergence of the people and the organization. A caution is offered here: personal and organizational goals cannot be artificially conjoined. If personal and professional goals are forced to match, then learning and growth opportunities through supervision or formalized staff development initiatives will begin to resemble the ill fated *one-size fits all* phenomenon that has historically plagued ineffective practices.

Through open dialogue and involvement in goal setting from both an organizational and a personal learning perspective, the organization and its people can move in a more purposeful manner. The principal can act as a sounding board for teachers as they review individual learning goals. The principal can also assist by openly listening and letting teachers talk about their goals and the importance of these goals in their professional development. Very few (if any) parameters should be im-

**FIGURE 1.2. TRACKING FACULTY GOALS**

| Teacher and Subject Area | Instructional Goal(s) | Classroom Procedure Goal(s) | Student Achievement Goal(s) | Professional Development Goal(s) |
|---|---|---|---|---|
| Arnot (English) | • closure on cooperative learning activities | • getting students into groups | • eliminate D grades by providing tutoring | • apply to a master's degree program |
| Baker (Spanish) | • learn to incorporate technology (Internet) in lessons | • getting students back on task while in cooperative learning groups | • how to grade student work while in cooperative learning groups | • attend a seminar or workshop on using technology<br>• read more about technology |
| Crawford (History) | • utilize more higher-ordered questioning techniques<br>• work on incorporating student responses in question and answer sessions | • work on getting class started without confrontational measures | • work on developing a fair makeup policy for missing homework assignments (for students who do not do their homework) | • learn more about the history fair sponsored by the local university |

posed on individual goal setting. The principal, through questioning, can lead teachers in defining their own goals and determining what is needed for achieving these goals.

## ATTRIBUTES OF GOALS

To assist the principal in leading his or her faculty through the goal-setting process, the attributes of goals as described by Lunenburg (1995) have been adapted to match the processes as they relate to supervision and staff development. Goals are:

- ◆ Specific: Goals are *specific* when they are clearly stated and understood. Specific goals are less likely to be ignored if each teacher is involved in generating his or her own professional development goals.

- ◆ Measurable: *Measurable* goals are precise. Although there are no absolutes in meeting goals, articulated goals can be measured over time. Through classroom observations and the discussions that follow, the supervisor and teacher are able to discuss progress toward achieving goals. Moreover, staff development activities tied to supervision can provide more relevancy to goals.

- ◆ Achievable: Goals are *achievable* if they are realistic. Effective principals encourage teachers to set goals that will make them *stretch* instead of allow them to coast. Growth occurs as a result of achievable goals. The effort needed to attain goal completion can inspire greater effort; unrealistic goals too far removed from reality are self-defeating.

- ◆ Relevant: Goals are *relevant* if they are viewed as important to the individual and to the organization. Superficial goals are often forgotten because they have no meaning to the individual or to the organization.

- ◆ Trackable: Goals need to be *trackable* in order to check progress. Goals should not be so numerous or complex that they confuse rather than direct the actions of those involved in accomplishing them.

"The essence of goal setting is regular task-relevant communication among members of the school organization....Collaboration in schools has been identified as the key schooling process variable for increasing the norms of student achievement" (Lunenburg, 1995, p. 41).

♦ Ongoing: Because professional development is an *ongoing* process, not all goals will be completed by the end of the year. Some goals are achieved over a longer period of time; other goals can be achieved more quickly.

Goals can become effective tools of leadership for a principal when they are phrased positively, defined precisely, prioritized, kept manageable, and evaluated regularly. The principal can extend the credibility of setting individual goals by building in a mechanism for teachers to self-evaluate their progress toward goal attainment. Some principals might prefer to hold a meeting with each teacher during the middle of the year. Others might prefer to ask teachers to identify markers of meeting their goals and just keep track of progress on their own. Regardless of the method chosen to track goal attainment throughout the year, it is absolutely necessary for the principal to meet with teachers at the end of the year so that together they can assess learning associated with their goals.

Goal attainment does not have to end with the year. Often teachers take the summer to reflect upon their year, attend workshops, reconfigure curriculum materials, and refine instructional approaches as a result of reflecting on the knowledge gained through practice. Hord and Cowan (1999) indicate a major shift in staff development tied to institutional development rests upon the teacher's involvement in understanding their own learning:

Increasingly, the focus is shifting to the teacher—to the teacher's knowledge, instructional strategies, and the way in which the teacher relates with the learner. Explicitly, we are focusing on what the teacher knows and can do, and on the teacher's continuing learning to improve his or her practice. (p. 44)

## DIALOGUE

Perhaps the strongest link between supervision and staff development is the dialogue between members of the learning community. Dialogue sustains conversation about practice over time. The importance of dialogue cannot be underrated. Discussion enhances thinking about teaching. Pajak (1993) suggests that teachers' own thinking brings about the most significant change in classroom practices.

## REFLECTION AND SELF-ANALYSIS PROMOTE CONSTRUCTING NEW KNOWLEDGE

Both supervision and staff development are concerned with teachers and administrators being able to make sense of their practices. Professional development activities, if they are to have any lasting impact, need to promote self-analysis and the construction of knowledge based on listening to one's own voice—through dialogue, discussion with peers, feedback, and reflection. Siens and Ebmeier (1996) believe that reflection is a multifaceted process where people rise "above the limits of tradition, technique, and authority to practice...in a manner that exhibits rational and intuitive thought" (p. 306). The value of reflection, according to McBride and Skau (1995), is "to lead teachers and administrators to greater self-awareness...and broader understanding of practice..." (p. 272).

Without reflection, supervision and staff development are ritualistic. Teachers need multiple opportunities to gain perspective on what they do in the classroom. O'Neil's (1998) discussion of the constructivist classroom focuses primarily on students; however, teachers and administrators can learn a valuable lesson:

> ...[P]eople learn by actively constructing knowledge, weighing new information against their previous understanding, thinking about and working through discrepancies (on their own and with others), and coming to a new understanding. (p. 51)

Sergiovanni and Starratt (1998) believe supervision can assist teachers to modify existing teaching patterns in ways that make sense to them. When teachers learn from their own practice, the classroom becomes an open-ended learning environment (Garman, 1982) that results in "analysis, interpretation, and decision making by the teacher" (Acheson & Gall, 1997, p. 18).

Lack of time during the day often limits opportunities for adults to discuss their work, let alone reflect on the impact of their instruction and other efforts on student learning. The block schedule will not provide more time per se; however, a block schedule can provide opportunity for longer periods of time for teachers to collaborate with one another. Reflection can occur in solitude in the quiet confines of an empty classroom or in the car on the way home from work. Moreover, reflection can occur while teaching, during a post-observation conference, with a trusted colleague, in writing, and even in large and small group discussions.

Huntress and Jones (1999) offer several possibilities for reflecting on practice with their Reflective Process Tools detailed in Figure 1.3. These processes can be tailored to the needs of teachers, and no one tool is championed over another. In fact, teachers might find themselves engaging in several of the reflective processes throughout the course of the year.

## FIGURE 1.3. REFLECTIVE PRACTICE TOOLS
## (DEVELOPED BY J. HUNTRESS AND L. JONES, 1999)

| *Reflective Process* | *Description and Source* |
|---|---|
| Photo Albums | Through a structured procedure, teachers and administrators describe their practice in terms of behavior, cause/effect relationship, rationale, and the like. These multiple descriptions create a "photo-album" of actions that are the focus of reflective discussion. |
| | Killion, J. P. & Todnem, G. R. (1991). A process for personal theory building. *Educational Leadership, 80*(3), 14–16. |
| Video Study Groups | Teachers tape lessons and then use these tapes as a springboard for collaborative reflections upon practice by a peer study group. |
| | Hassler, S. S. & Collins, A. M. (1993). *Using collaborative reflection to support changes in classroom practice.* Paper presented at the Annual Meeting of the American Educational Research Association (Atlanta, GA: April 12–16, 1993). |
| Action Research | Classroom-based studies, initiated and conducted by teachers, form the basis of action research. Action research affords teachers the opportunity to collect, analyze, and then reflect on the meaning of data. |
| | Bennett, C. K. (1994). Promoting teaching reflection through action research: What do teachers think? *Journal of Staff Development, 15*(1), 34–38. |

| Reflective Process | Description and Source |
|---|---|
| Thinking Frameworks | Thinking frameworks provide a common language and basis from which reflection can occur. Cook writes that models of thinking, such as Gardner's Multiple Intelligences, and Martinello and Cook's Habits of Mind, can aid in the inquiry process of clinical supervision by providing common understandings from which to work. Cook refers to such models as a "variety of lenses to view the world of the classroom and gain new insights into its workings" (p. 50).<br><br>Cook, G. E. (1996). Using clinical supervision to promote inquiry. *Journal of Staff Development, 17*(4), 46–50. |
| Dewey's Reflective Framework | Teachers move through Dewey's five-step problem-posing process:<br>1. Felt Difficulty<br>2. Location and Definition<br>3. Suggestions of Possible Solution<br>4. Development by Reasoning of the Bearings of the Suggestion<br>5. Further Observation and Experimentation leading to its Acceptance or Rejection.<br><br>After going through the five-step process, teachers can better reflect upon classroom experiences while generating solutions to problems of practice.<br><br>Yusko, B. P. (1997). *Planning and enacting reflective talk among interns What is the problem?* Paper presented at the Annual Meeting of the Association of Teacher Educators (St. Louis, MO: February 24–28, 1997). |

| Reflective Process | Description and Source |
|---|---|
| Journals | Teachers make journal entries focused on beliefs, knowledge, observations, and actions related to teaching.<br><br>Kasten, B. J. & Ferraro, J. M. (1995). *A case study: Helping pre-service teachers internalize the interconnectedness of believing, knowing, seeing, and doing.* Paper presented at the Annual Meeting of the American Educational Research Association (San Francisco: April 18–22, 1995). |
| Dialogue Journals | Teachers/interns keep journals to record classroom experiences, ideas, and questions. Mentors respond through commentary, or "dialogue," within these journals.<br><br>Krol, C. A. (1996). *Pre-service teacher education students' reflective writing and teachers' comments.* Paper presented at the Annual Meeting of the Association of Teacher Educators (St. Louis, MO: February 24–28, 1997). |
| Think Alouds | Mentors model reflection-in-action as they talk through a lesson. As the lesson progresses, mentors articulate their decision-making framework.<br><br>Loughran, J. (1995). *Practicing what I preach: Modeling reflective practice to student teachers.* Paper presented at the Annual Meeting of the American Educational Research Association (San Francisco: April 18–22, 1995). |
| Zen | Mentor teachers practice the "mindful awareness of the present moment" to encourage reflection-in-action among pre-service teachers.<br><br>Tremmel, R. (1993). Zen and the art of reflective practice in teacher education. *Harvard Educational Review, 63*(1), 443–458. |

| Reflective Process | Description and Source |
|---|---|
| Cognitive Coaching | Cognitive coaching is a plan designed to "stimulate collaborative efforts" (p. 5) in the analysis of practice. Thought clusters, such as metacognition and dissonance, are used to help teachers become more aware of the thinking upon which their teaching is based.<br><br>Costa, A. L. & Garmston, R. J. (1994). *Cognitive coaching: Foundation for Renaissance schools.* Norwood, MA: Christopher-Gordon. |
| Teaching Dialogues | This staff development model is structured to engage four or five participants in inquiry, reflection, and discussion on a scheduled basis. Creative restructuring of the school day provides time for teacher dialogues.<br><br>Arnold, G. C. (1995). Teacher dialogues: A constructivist model of staff development. *Journal of Staff Development, 16*(4), 34–38. |
| Critical Incidents | Teachers write autobiographies describing their own experiences of school, then write about a "critical incident" from daily practice in their own teaching experience. In follow-up discussions, participants compare the two documents to discover their assumptions about teaching.<br><br>Kennedy, R. L. & Wyrick, A. M. (1995). *Teaching as reflective practice.* Paper presented at the Annual Meeting of the Mid-South Educational Research Association (Biloxi, MS: 1995). |

The tools annotated by Huntress and Jones can assist teachers in reflecting on their practices and on the impact that these practices have on student learning. However, time purposefully planned during the workday needs to be found. In a block schedule, several strategies can be used to find time in the day for teachers to analyze and reflect on practices, whether alone or in small groups. The principal's task is to help find and then to protect this time.

## FEEDBACK

Supervision and staff development are most helpful when feedback is continuous and supportive of what the teacher is trying to accomplish. Feedback that comes from a variety of sources through more collaborative applications of supervision (coaching) is more valid than from a single source (e.g., only the administrator assigned to supervise or evaluate the teacher).

If teachers believe they can achieve a valued outcome that is relevant to their teaching situation, they will sustain the effort and energy required to practice a new learning technique. Communication, specifically feedback, will only be heard if the person giving the feedback has credibility and a sincere desire to provide support. Trust is the cornerstone of effective communication. Pascarelli and Ponticell (1994) provide samples of what they refer to as *trust-blocking responses*. Figure 1.4 highlights trust-blocking responses to avoid in order to foster more collaborative feedback.

## REFINEMENT OF PRACTICE

Often, after a staff development activity or post-observation conference, teachers return to their classrooms and leave at the door what they have learned. Lost are the opportunities for the teacher to implement skills within the complexities of the classroom. Teachers need time to conceptualize how a practice or application of a technique will be implemented in their classrooms. Without a mechanism in place to provide ongoing support and feedback about instructional practices, modifications are not likely to be forthcoming. In a block schedule, teachers are asked to modify their instructional practices. Without opportunities for refinement, modification of instructional practices is difficult to achieve.

Secondary classrooms are prone to be more isolated due to the subject specialization that is required to teach at this level. Marsh and Daro (1999) offer two specific strategies for professional development at the high school level that can be transferred to use in a block schedule: "…Professional development

## FIGURE 1.4. TRUST-BLOCKING RESPONSES
## (DEVELOPED BY J. T. PASCARELLI AND J. A. PONTICELL, 1994)

♦ *Evaluation*—Phrases such as the following tend to evoke defensiveness: "You should…," "Your responsibility here is…," "You are wrong about…"

♦ *Advice Giving*—Advice is best given if requested; responses such as "Why don't you just…," "You would be better off…," or "Your best action is…" can go in one ear and out the other if unsolicited.

♦ *Topping*—"That's nothing, you should have seen…," "Well, in my class…," "When that happened to me…," "You think you have it bad, well…" are phrases of one-upmanship. They shift attention from the person who wants to be listened to and leaves him/her feeling unimportant.

♦ *Diagnosing*—Phrases that tell others what they feel (e.g., "What you need is…," "The reason you feel that way is…," "You really don't mean that…," "Your problem is…") can create two-edged sword, either leaving the person feeling pressured if the speaker is wrong or feeling exposed or "caught" if the speaker is right.

♦ *Warning*—"You had better…," "If you don't…," "You have to…," or "You must…" can produce resentment, resistance, or rebellion if the recipient feels the "finger of blame" is being pointed in his/her direction.

♦ *Lecturing*—"Don't you realize…," "Here is where you are wrong…," "The facts simply prove…," or "Yes, but…," can make the person feel inferior or defensive. Full, descriptive data and problem-solving questioning allow the individual to make logical decisions for him or herself.

♦ *Devaluation*—"It's not so bad…," "Don't worry…," "You'll get over it…," or "Oh, you really don't feel that way…" take away or deny the feelings of the speaker. Conveying nonacceptance of the speaker's feelings creates a lack of trust, feelings of inferiority or fault, and fear of risk taking.

networks linked to subject matter and student performance, and within-school lesson study groups" (p. 83). With an eye on gains in student learning, the power of cadres of professional network members working across subject and grade levels helps "...link teachers who are working in a similar subject area towards helping students reach the same or very similar student performance success" (p. 84).

Subject matter networks as envisioned by Marsh and Daro (1999) can be developed with the assistance of the principal. Principals can help foster the work of professional subject matter networks by:

♦ Providing release time during the day (paraprofessionals can be utilized to cover duty periods);

♦ Assisting teachers in obtaining data about student performance so they can track results about what instructional techniques and modifications in curriculum arrangement produce what gains;

♦ Reconfiguring faculty meetings so subject matter networks can meet;

♦ Finding resources needed for teachers to accomplish their work; and,

♦ Staying out of the way of teachers and their work.

The power of subject matter networks is that teachers "...can also gauge the success of their professional development by looking at the impact on student performance" (Marsh & Daro, 1999, p. 84). Teachers, when they collaborate with one another, are able to generate more alternatives, take more calculated risks, and see more clearly the results of their work. Ponticell (1995) believes that, "sustained, substantive, and structured collegial interactions enhance mutuality and support risk taking" (p. 17).

Chapter 4 discusses curriculum development designs and auditing techniques. The principal is encouraged to consult this chapter to examine auditing techniques. The results of curricular, instructional, and assessment audits can complement supervisory and staff development processes.

## THE CONDITIONS NEEDED TO FOSTER MORE COLLABORATIVE, PROFESSIONAL INTERACTION

### CREATE A CLIMATE FOR PROFESSIONAL GROWTH

Schools with a positive learning climate value and uphold norms of collegiality among the people (e.g., teachers, parents, students, and administrators) who comprise the school community. According to the work of Little, schools that promote continuous improvement are engaged in:

+ Frequent, continuous, and increasingly concrete talk about teaching practice;
+ Frequent observations of each other's teaching, accompanied by useful critiques;
+ Planning, designing, researching, preparing, and evaluating instructional materials together; and,
+ Taking responsibility of teaching and practicing teaching with one another. (Adapted from Howey & Vaughan, 1983, pp. 107–108)

If professional growth opportunities are to have an effect on teachers and their learning, these opportunities need to be relevant. Relevancy is more easily realized if supervision and staff development activities are embedded in the daily work of teaching and supported by the organizational structures of the school. In addition to relevancy, teachers need time to be actively involved in charting new ways to apply lessons learned through supervision and staff development *in their classrooms*. Job-embedded supervision and staff development are addressed extensively in Chapter 6.

### GETTING SMART ABOUT LEARNING

Most school systems are involved in studying the dimensions and design of a block schedule the year before implementation. Some school systems are ready to launch a block schedule; others, however, may not be so ready. Moving to a block schedule requires that the organization *get smart* by learning how to learn. In smart schools, effective principals begin supervision and staff development for the block *before* implementation. Supervision and staff development become the mechanism for implementing change. The importance of the interconnected nature of the learning that needs to be accomplished by both the organization and its people cannot be underestimated. Learning drives change.

## ORGANIZATIONAL LEARNING

Botkin, Elmandjra, and Malitza (1979) (as cited in Bennis (1989)) identify three types of learning that organizations and people encounter when change occurs: *maintenance learning, shock learning,* and *innovative learning.* Although these types of learning were originally applied to the corporate sector, they are worth examining within the context of a school setting in the block or in the process of implementing a block schedule. While getting ready to implement a block schedule, multiple levels of learning and change will occur: the day-to-day operations (e.g., passing periods), the structure of the classroom (e.g., longer class sessions), and instructional practices (e.g., multiple instructional practices in a single block).

*Maintenance learning* "…is the type of learning designed to maintain an existing system" (Botkin et al. (1979) cited in Bennis (1989), p. 75). From an instructional perspective, it is safe and comforting for teachers to embrace the strategies used before the block. Although these instructional strategies were effective, they will need modification for a block schedule. Curriculum will need to be modified to take advantage of the extended time afforded by a block. Bennis (1989) believes that maintenance learning is "less learning" (p. 75) and more concerned in embracing the status quo. If instructional practices utilized before the block schedule are merely transplanted to the block schedule, then learning is "less."

For supervision and staff development in a block to be effective, teachers and students need to go beyond just maintaining a new system with things that worked before the block schedule. Just because a block schedule extends learning periods, does not mean that teachers will automatically change their instructional practices, that teaching and learning are being enhanced, or that the features of the block schedule are being utilized to assist students in making gains in their learning.

From an organizational perspective, the very structure of the school day itself will change. These changes can throw the school system into *shock learning* that "...occurs when events overwhelm people" (Botkin et al. (1979) cited in Bennis (1989), p. 75). Shock learning is, perhaps, the least effective type of learning due to the fear and anxiety associated with adapting new ways of getting things done. This type of learning can be avoided if:

♦ Teachers are involved in staff development prior to the block;

♦ Teachers are involved in ongoing staff development as the block is being implemented; and,

♦ Instructional supervision changes to meet the needs of teachers as they grapple with refining and learning new instructional practices. (Zepeda, 1999b)

*Innovative learning* is powerful because it prepares people for the future (Bennis, 1989). According to Bennis, innovative learning includes:

♦ Anticipation—being active, imaginative rather than passive, and habitual;

♦ Communication—learning by listening to others; and,

♦ Participation—shaping events, rather than being shaped by them. (pp. 76–77)

The move to a block schedule can be a renewing experience if the entire community works toward a common goal—the improvement of the learning environment. Through open exchanges and group problem solving, the members of the school community can learn from one another. It will be through the group's energy and momentum for change that a more creative learning environment can be shaped.

## ENLARGING THE POWER BASE FOR LEARNING

Learning to teach should be viewed as a process that continues throughout one's entire career. Teachers should participate in determining the direction of their professional growth. Principals must be both leaders and followers (Sergiovanni, 1992) if others are to be empowered to grow. Professional development, driven by all members assuming equal responsibility for growth, creates a collective involvement, replete with a collective energy and focus—synergy (Senge, 1990). Supervision and staff development in a block schedule needs to be rethought if faculty development and school improvement are to be achieved. "Of the many roles the principal must play, the role…of staff development deserves the highest priority" (McCall, 1997, p. 23). As staff developer and supervisor, the principal realizes that "the actual process of learning that teachers go through is as important, if not more important, than the teaching they do in the classroom. *Students learn only from teachers who are themselves in the process of learning*" (McCall, 1997, p. 23, emphasis in the original).

### ASSESSING TEACHER WILLINGNESS TO LEARN

People learn at their own rate. Workplace conditions, such as the relationship between the administration and teachers and the norms of collegiality, effect learning. Learning cannot be mandated nor can it be imposed. The astute principal realizes that adults, very much like children, learn at different rates, and they respond to learning opportunities differently. This, at first blush, might appear to be a demeaning perspective. Zepeda (1999a) indicates that principals can be more effective if they know their teachers as *learners* just like effective teachers know when to shift instruction and learning activities to meet the individual and collective needs of students in the classroom. From this perspective, the principal is encouraged to view the school as a classroom where all members are engaged in learning individually and collectively. The principal is encouraged to assess current practices by examining:

♦ *Learning:* Do teachers on their own seek out learning opportunities offered at the site, district, or externally (graduate school, local and national conferences and workshops)?

- *Sharing:* Do teachers share their knowledge and expertise with other teachers? Do they have a forum for *bringing home* what they have learned in professional development activities?
- *Reflecting and Discussing:* Do teachers openly discuss what they have learned or what they are in the process of discovering about their own teaching practices?
- *Examining the Talk Over Time:* Are discussions held over a sustained period? One-time discussions, like one-shot staff development *events*, are equally useless in promoting professional growth.
- *Reading the Word:* Are books, professional journals, and technology utilized as resources? Are these resources readily available to teachers and professional staff (e.g., secretaries and custodians)? (p. 23)

After examining these conditions, the principal can further reflect on his/her own supervisory and staff development practices and how teachers are involved in these practices. For example, if teachers are encouraged to and are willingly involved in visiting each other's classrooms, learning through collegial types of supervision (e.g., peer coaching and videotape analysis) can be more meaningful than administratively imposed and bureaucratically controlled supervision, which is more concerned with teacher evaluation. Teachers will bring to the block schedule a wealth of information about teaching and learning. Through supervision and staff development geared to building on effective instructional practices, teachers will be able to seize learning opportunities for themselves and their students—if people are valued.

## VALUE PEOPLE

People—teachers, custodians, volunteers, students, and parents—are the school. Teachers often spend more time with children than parents. Teachers, by the very nature of their work, are shaping and molding our future. This is an awesome responsibility; therefore, teachers need to strive to "continually improve performance and enhance value to shareholders"

(Pasternack & Viscio, 1998, p. 67). Value is not necessarily what an individual can do for the organization; but, rather, what each individual can contribute to the other lives in the school.

To be a contributing member, teachers need to feel valued and appreciated for who they are and what strengths and talents they bring to the school. Teachers need to know that their work is appreciated, valued, and serves a purpose. Teachers need to feel connected to others in an environment that affirms their efforts.

To meet these needs, effective principals build and support strengths and provide proactive assistance when and where needed through innovative learning opportunities provided through staff development and supervision. Special care is needed by the principal to avoid presenting supervision and staff development as a means to *correct* a weakness. Supervision and staff development designed from a deficit point of view will accomplish little but to create low morale among teachers.

## PROVIDE COHERENCE

The principal can create momentum for learning by serving as the glue to connect people and their efforts to improve the learning environment of the school. Principals can achieve this by forming "new people partnerships" (Pasternack & Viscio, 1998, p. 67) where coherence:

> ...is the glue that binds the various pieces, enabling them to act as one. It includes a broad range of processes. It begins with a shared vision and shared set of values, and expands to include numerous linkages across the company. (p. 61)

Glickman, Gordon, and Ross-Gordon (1998) believe that supervision is the "glue" that connects all learning opportunities which includes, for them and others (e.g., Blase & Blase, 1998), staff development.

Coherence is essential to successful professional development. The processes inherent to supervision and staff development can unify efforts and enhance outcomes for both students and teachers. By purposefully finding linkages between supervision and staff development (peer coaching, mentoring, and study groups), a powerful opportunity exists for the principal to provide coherence between these efforts. Learning can become more meaningful because of this unity of effort and purpose. Figure 1.5, developed by Zepeda (1994), illustrates the unity of purpose between supervision and staff development.

During the move to a block schedule, the principal's attention needs to be focused on the quality of instruction. With confidence, the principal needs to be ready to shift organizational structures (e.g., procedures and processes) in such a way that teachers can focus on learning—their own and that of their students. Principals, by the very nature of their job descriptions, are responsible for the establishment and maintenance of the overall educational operation of the school. Sergiovanni (1996) believes school leaders should be interested in:

> ...Serving the common good, in ministering to the needs of the school, and in providing the oversight that protects the school and keeps it on a true course, clarifying purposes, promoting unity, and helping people to understand the problems they face and to find solutions. (p. xvi)

Numerous changes will occur before and during the implementation of a block schedule. If detailed attention is not given to the changes associated with a block schedule, then the organization will be in a continual state of flux, band-aiding the system with short-term solutions to issues that can have long-term impact. By examining organizational structures, the school community will be in a better position to examine block scheduling before implementation.

## ORGANIZATIONAL STRUCTURES IN THE BLOCK THAT NEED CAREFUL ATTENTION

Before implementing a block schedule, decisions need to be made: Which block configuration should be adopted? What are the learning needs of students? How will these needs be met? What types of curricular and instructional modifications need to be made? The reader is encouraged to examine the various

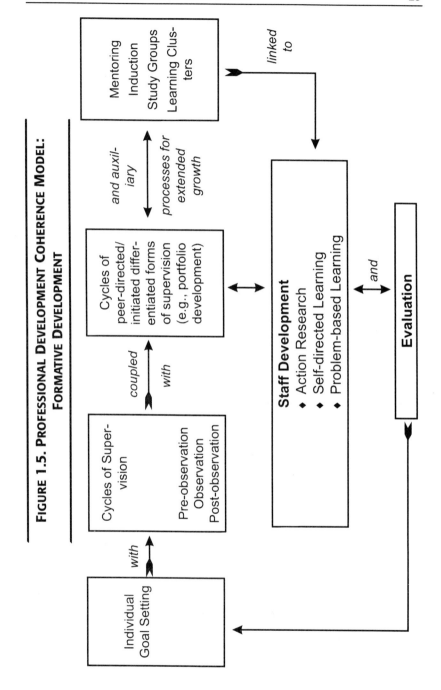

FIGURE 1.5. PROFESSIONAL DEVELOPMENT COHERENCE MODEL: FORMATIVE DEVELOPMENT

block configurations presented in Chapter 2 before adopting a block schedule. For the principal, the big question should be what types of staff development will benefit the faculty in making these decisions. Before the structures of the school can be examined, the principal is encouraged to build a vision for the block.

## CREATE A VISION FOR THE BLOCK

Teachers need to know that there is a reason for moving to a block schedule, and that the leadership of the school has a long-term commitment to this change. Effective principals involve people in adding form to the vision, but teachers need to know that a vision with an initial roadmap to get people organized and onboard exists. Without a vision and a timeline for implementation, teachers will put scant effort into the initiative.

The principal articulates the vision. Teachers and others in the community launch the vision. Goals, objectives, and some target dates might need to be adjusted as teachers put shape to the vision. As indicated earlier, it will be the teachers who will carry the *plan* to fruition. Therefore, special care and support will need to be provided to teachers.

## REACH OUT TO TEACHERS

Be realistic and expect faculty to have differing ideas about the block and its application in *their* school. There are two types of tension: healthy and unhealthy. Differing ideas can create a *healthy tension* and spark lively discussion. Healthy tension can move people and the structures of the school toward innovative learning (Bennis, 1989) where the status quo can be challenged, and where the organization can move forward in attaining long- and short-term goals. On the other hand, unhealthy tension, if not addressed, can fragment teachers into splinter groups. Excessive negativity drains energy and can dampen momentum.

The principal can combat unhealthy tension by:

- ♦ Letting people express their concerns privately and in group settings without fear of retribution;

- Finding opportunities to strike up conversations with those who are not enthusiastic about moving to a block schedule;

- Involving people in committee/team work (e.g., staff development) that taps into their strengths;

- Demonstrating an absolute commitment to the goal of implementing a block schedule; and,

- Building momentum for a block schedule through a formalized staff development plan geared toward getting the school to the block.

## COMMUNICATE WITH STAKEHOLDERS

Time spent communicating with stakeholders from the start of planning for a block will help ease the transition to the thinking and work needed to implement the block. This upfront time helps keep parents updated on progress. Parent newsletters and special mailings are a solid start. Other communication channels can be used:

- *Parent Groups*—PTA/PTO and other parent groups often meet monthly at the school. The principal is encouraged to seek teacher volunteers to present information at their meetings. Simple handouts can assist in communicating important information.

- *Special Meetings*—Arrange a special meeting in the evening for all parents, or consider a special meeting time during parent-teacher conferences.

- *Media Coverage*—Invite the editor or the education reporter from the local newspaper to visit the school. An article on the block schedule will communicate to even larger audiences. Utilize television if the district has its own cable station.

- *Board of Education Meetings*—Teachers and the principal can prepare a formal presentation for a monthly board meeting. Include students and parents in the presentation.

- *Student Meetings*—Students are among the biggest stakeholders in the change to a block schedule, and they, too, need to be kept informed and involved in the process. Concerns that revolve around course selection, activity and sport commitments before and after school, school starting and ending times, and passing period length are examples of what interests students. Input from students can provide valuable insight concerning obstacles that need attention while planning for the block.

♦ *Civic Group Meetings*—The business sector of the community needs to keep updated on changes because it is this sector that employs students after and before school. This sector also provides services to the community (e.g., restaurants, convenience stores), and they need to plan for possible changes in patterns (e.g., lunch-break times, school beginning and ending times). With the increase in service learning initiatives, community service programs (both mandatory and voluntary), school-to-work initiatives, and school-business partnerships, local agencies and establishments have a vested interest in school initiatives.

## PARENTAL INVOLVEMENT AND THE BLOCK

Perhaps no group of stakeholders has a greater interest in student success than do parents. In response to this interest, many districts and states mandate that teacher staff development include training on how to involve parents. However, a great potential for learning and growth is lost if schools fail to show parents how to become involved in their child's education. What good is training teachers how to work with parents, while omitting parents from the process?

### STAFF DEVELOPMENT FOR PARENTS

Staff development needs to be provided *for* parents not merely *about* parents. In the context of a school moving toward implementing a block schedule, staff development for parents:

♦ Generates additional input into the decision concerning which type of block schedule to implement;

♦ Provides a forum for parents to voice concerns about block scheduling to teachers and administrators; and,

♦ Furnishes teachers and administrators an opportunity to recruit parents for active participation in the learning community.

A comprehensive staff development plan for parents should include diverse learning activities that:

♦ Introduce parents to block scheduling;

♦ Identify issues that teachers and administrators expect block scheduling to address;

♦ Invite parents to learn how the implementation of a block schedule will effect their child's education; and,

♦ Involve parents in such activities as action research while monitoring their child's progress.

## INTRODUCING PARENTS TO THE BLOCK

Schools need to involve parents in the pre-planning stages of investigating the block so that parents feel they are an integral part of the process. Informing parents and seeking their input can be an effective method of proactive problem solving. Principals should be prepared to answer these questions:

♦ What is block scheduling?

♦ Why is our school considering the block?

♦ What types of block schedules are being considered?

♦ What does this mean for my child?

Tips for conducting introductory parent meetings include:

♦ Hold at least two introductory meetings, varying the time and day. This will assist parents to find a convenient time for attending.

♦ Publish the agenda prior to the meeting. This lets parents know how their time will be spent.

- ◆ Prepare handouts that describe the proposed new schedule and the role of parents in its success.

- ◆ Involve business and teacher leaders in the meeting to build a sense of community.

- ◆ Invite the local press to cover the meeting. Newspaper, radio, and television reports can help reach those parents who were unable to attend.

Figure 1.6 offers a sample agenda for an introductory meeting.

---

### FIGURE 1.6. AGENDA FOR AN
### "INTRODUCTION TO THE BLOCK" PARENT MEETING

---

I.   Welcome and Introductions

II.  What is a block schedule and what will it look like?

III. What does this mean for your child?

IV.  How you can help…

V.   Feedback (Questions and Answers)

---

### INVITING PARENTS TO EXPERIENCE THE BLOCK

Another important phase of staff development for parents is allowing them to experience firsthand how block scheduling will effect their child's education. Several strategies can help to accomplish this. First, recruit parents to host *study nights* in their homes. A study night consists of a group of parents and students working on homework assignments together with a teacher. This type of event gives teachers an opportunity to become better acquainted with parents while helping to familiarize students and parents with ways in which homework might change in a block schedule. Another variation of the study night is to conduct it at the school where several teachers might be present to assist.

*Mini Nights* provide an additional mechanism for acquainting parents with the block. A Mini Night is an open house in which parents follow their child's schedule for an entire, but abbreviated, school day. Mini Nights should be held near the beginning of the school year to get parents involved from the start. Tips for organizing Mini Nights are:

- Begin publicity early! Give parents plenty of time to arrange schedules so they can attend;
- Have copies of student schedules and campus maps available for parents to pick up;
- Start the Mini Night with a general assembly to acquaint parents with faculty and to give parents necessary instructions;
- Use the usual bell system to signal the beginning and ending of each "class" period;
- Be sure each teacher has a well-developed presentation for each group of parents that consists of a summary of classroom rules and routines, a mini-lesson relevant to the class, and a short question and answer period; and,
- Be sure there are plenty of people available (e.g., *all* non-teaching staff, honor society, or service club members) to help parents navigate the building.

For parents that desire an even more realistic experience with the block, provide opportunities to *shadow* their children during a normal school day. Shadowing refers to a parent accompanying his/her child throughout a regular school day. Because some sites use shadowing as a consequence in their discipline plans, allow parents to visit classrooms other than those that include their child if they wish.

### INVOLVEMENT: PARENTS AS ACTION RESEARCHERS

In too many school districts, parents remain an underutilized resource. Parents need to be seen through a new lens: as action researchers. By tracking their children's grades, time spent on homework for each course, and numbers of quizzes and tests taken, a sizable data set can be assembled that can be used to address myriad research questions. For example, a tenth grade history teacher could, as a result of a parent-teacher conference, discover the benefit of researching the relationship between instructional strategies used in class and the types and amount of homework assigned. By devising a simple data collection instrument for parents to track what homework assignments their child completes, the teacher involves parents as action researchers. Encourage submission of the completed tracking forms by counting them as a homework assignment. Following analysis and interpretation of the data, the teacher could share the results with colleagues at a faculty meeting and with parents at the next parent-teacher conference night. Results could also be shared through the school's Web page or, where available, the district's cable television station.

---

**BUILDING BLOCK:**
**STEPS FOR CONDUCTING ACTION**
**RESEARCH**

1. Select a focus.
2. Collect data.
3. Analyze and interpret data.
4. Take action.

---

## STRUCTURAL AREAS IN NEED OF ORGANIZATIONAL SUPERVISION

The first year in a block schedule can be taxing for everyone in the building (teachers, students, and custodians), those served by the school (students, parents, and community members), and those who work in auxiliary capacities (bus drivers and cafeteria workers). All the parts of the school must work together; otherwise, the system itself will be thrown into shock learning. An organization in shock-learning mode often suffers from decisions made to *patch* fragmented parts or by people who do not have enough information to make sound decisions that can stay made.

## INFRASTRUCTURE OF THE SCHOOL

It is amazing to think of the daily operations of a school that are taken for granted until a change topples the system. Areas of the school that will need organizational supervision before implementing a block include:

♦ Traffic patterns in the hallways before and after school and during passing periods;

♦ Bus schedules (regular and extracurricular);

♦ Cafeteria (lunch period times, the number of lunch periods offered);

♦ Facilities (maintenance—daily and long-term schedules; rental and usage after school);

♦ Assemblies (scheduling patterns);

♦ Standardized and districtwide testing programs; and,

♦ Availability of resources (books, computer lab/ classroom usage).

## THE MASTER SCHEDULE

The master schedule and scheduling students for courses will need much attention. The principal will need to ensure that electives are offered across both semesters. Some courses, such as band, journalism (newspaper and yearbook), and advanced-level foreign languages, might need to run all year in a traditional format. Advanced placement courses might also need special consideration when developing the master schedule. Avoid the scheduling trap of trying to make too many exceptions to the block. Suddenly, the block is no longer a block.

## FORM ACTION RESEARCH TEAMS, LEARNING CLUSTERS, AND FOCUS GROUPS

As soon as the decision has been made to move to a block, solicit volunteers from the faculty to study research and evaluation report findings on the impact of the block and on what staff development activities were most valuable to schools that have already moved to the block. Enlist the support of the librarian/media specialist who can lead the way to accessing information through electronic searches. Technology teachers might help with searching the net for information on the block. Several school districts support Web pages. Schools often chronicle their experiences with the block (pre- and post-implementation), and report the results of program evaluation on their Web pages. In addition, there are many professional organizations that publish information relevant to block scheduling, such as evaluation results, research, articles, and URLs to other Web sites. Chapter 6 details the concepts of action research. To ensure a successful move to a block schedule, the organization as well as its people must be readied.

---

**BUILDING BLOCK:
WEB SITES ON BLOCK SCHEDULING**

The following Web sites can provide information about Block Scheduling:

♦ The National Staff Development Council: www.nsdc.org
♦ The Association for Supervision and Curriculum Development: www.ascd.org
♦ Eye on Education: www.eyeoneducation.com
♦ Corwin Press: www.corwinpress.com
♦ National Association of Secondary School Principals (NASSP): www.nassp.org

---

## SUMMARY

This chapter provides an exploration of the principal's role in providing staff development and supervision in the movement toward a block schedule. It is the principal who is responsible for creating the conditions for implementing a block schedule. However, the principal cannot accomplish all of the preparation alone. Effective principals obtain the support of all stakeholders, especially teachers. Many changes will be made as a result of moving to the block. Perhaps the biggest change is the role of the principal in providing supervision and staff development. No system can sustain change over an extended period of time without changes made in supervisory and staff development practices that promote growth and learning. A block schedule is no exception.

## SUGGESTED READINGS

Ackerman, R. H., Donaldson, G. A., & van der Bogert, R. (1996). *Making sense as a school leader: Persisting questions, creative opportunities.* San Francisco: Jossey-Bass.

Blase, J., & Blase, J. (1998). *Handbook of instructional leadership: How really good principals promote teaching and learning.* Thousand Oaks, CA: Corwin Press.

Blase, J., & Blase, J. (1997). *The fire is back! Principals sharing school governance.* Thousand Oaks, CA: Corwin Press.

Crow, G. M., Matthews, L. J., & McCleary, L. E. (1996). *Leadership: A relevant and realistic role for principals.* Larchmont, NY: Eye on Education.

Glickman, C. D., Gordon, S. P., & Ross-Gordon, J. M. (1998). *Supervision of instruction: A developmental approach* (4th ed.). Boston: Allyn and Bacon.

Zepeda, S. J. (1999a). *Staff development: Practices that promote leadership in learning communities.* Larchmont, NY: Eye on Education.

# 2

# REINVENTING TIME: LOOKING AT THE BLOCK

## CHAPTER OBJECTIVES

- Identify different types of block schedules and the strengths and weaknesses of each.
- Examine brain and intelligence research and its relevance to teaching in the block.
- Describe the ways block scheduling impacts teaching and learning.

As the twenty-first century approaches, public schools are grappling with the age-old problem of how best to utilize limited resources to accommodate ever increasing needs. In addition to core instruction, schools provide a myriad of services for students: counseling; special, gifted, and vocational education; fine arts; athletics; and industrial arts programs, to name a few. Graduates must be prepared for the most technologically advanced world in history.

Perhaps the most difficult resource to harness is time. An increasing number of schools have attempted to transform themselves into more efficient learning organizations by rearranging the *boundaries* of time. Unfortunately, time management, by itself, is not enough. In *First Things First*, Covey, Merrill, and Merrill state:

> Time management...sounds good. It gives the promise of achievement, a sense of hope. But it doesn't deliver...More than evolution, we need a revolution. We need to move beyond time management to life leadership...based on paradigms that will create quality-of-life results. (1995, p. 31)

How the boundaries of time are redefined must be decided by examining the existing structures of the school day and year. All school cultures are unique; thus, the schedule design should consistently complement all facets of the school. For innovative schedules to be successful, schools need to do more than just alter the boundaries of time. *What occurs within the newly defined time blocks must also change.* Teachers need the opportunity to learn and implement new practices.

The move to a new schedule involves more than a shift in hours and minutes. Successful schools on block schedules experience a shift in paradigms. The paradigm of individuals is replaced with *connectedness*. Covey and associates describe "connectedness" as the transition from the "independent paradigm" to the "interdependent paradigm" (Covey, et al., 1995, pp. 198–200).

# BLOCKS, BLOCKS, AND MORE BLOCKS

The first step in any journey is the selection of a destination. The decision to investigate block scheduling can seem deceptively simple. Mapping the course may, at times, remind the traveler of negotiating a maze. As with any educational reform, even the most straightforward of concepts can become complex when adapted to the individual needs of schools.

The traditional schedule, made up of 7 to 8 classes of 45 to 55 minutes each per day, was developed in 1892 by the National Education Association's Committee of Ten. Block scheduling traces its history to the late 1950s and the work of J. Lloyd Trump. Trump's Flexible Modular System was designed to substitute modules of differing amounts of time for the unyielding class periods of the traditional school day (Canady & Rettig, 1995). By the mid-1980s, three main varieties of block schedules emerged: *accelerated*, *alternating*, and *Copernican*. For the convenience of the reader, the following descriptions of the most common types of block schedules, with advantages and disadvantages of each, are offered.

## THE ACCELERATED BLOCK

The most common form of the accelerated block is the *4 x 4 block*. The school day is divided into four roughly equivalent blocks of time, usually 80 to 90 minutes each. This schedule is similar to a university schedule in that students complete their first set of courses at the end of the fall semester and begin new classes in January. In a 4 x 4 block, teachers usually teach three blocks per day and have one block for planning. Figure 2.1 depicts a 4 x 4 student schedule.

Another popular form of the accelerated block, the *trimester*, divides the school year into three terms instead of two. Each 60-day trimester is divided into three class periods of 110 to 130 minutes each. Figure 2.2 depicts a student schedule on a trimester block.

## FIGURE 2.1. STUDENT SCHEDULE IN THE 4 x 4 BLOCK

|  | *Fall* | *Spring* |
|---|---|---|
| *Block 1* | Algebra II | Vocational Agriculture I |
| *Block 2* | English II | World History |
| *Block 3* | Computer Science I | Art I |
| *Block 4* | German II | Biology I |

## FIGURE 2.2. STUDENT TRIMESTER SCHEDULE

|  | *Trimester 1* | *Trimester 2* | *Trimester 3* |
|---|---|---|---|
| *Block 1* | English I | Physical Science | American History |
| *Block 2* | Vocal Music | Industrial Arts | Geometry |
| *Block 3* | Algebra I | Athletics | French I |

In the trimester system, lunch periods are usually embedded in block 2. A third of the student population has lunch before class, a third after class, and the final group has their second class *sandwiched* around a lunch period in the middle of the second time block.

Another variation of the accelerated block is the *quarter on–quarter off* system. The school year is divided into four 45-day quarters that are designed to enable different students varying time to complete courses. For example, one student may take one quarter to complete Algebra I, and another student can have two or more quarters to complete the same course. The student who quickly completes Algebra I may then begin a new course (Canady & Rettig, 1995).

A fourth variation of the accelerated block is the rotating block. Using this type of schedule, schools rotate the time of day in which each class meets. Figure 2.3 depicts a student rotating 4 x 4 schedule.

### FIGURE 2.3. STUDENT SCHEDULE ON THE ROTATING 4 x 4 BLOCK

|  | *Monday* | *Tuesday* | *Wednesday* | *Thursday* | *Friday* |
|---|---|---|---|---|---|
| *Block 1* | English I | US History | Algebra I | Chorus | English I |
| *Block 2* | Chorus | English I | US History | Algebra I | Chorus |
| *Block 3* | Algebra I | Chorus | English I | US History | Algebra I |
| *Block 4* | US History | Algebra I | Chorus | English I | US History |

Rotating allows all classes to experience the benefits associated with different time periods during the day. This prevents any course from always bearing the burden presented by different time blocks. For example, an English teacher does not spend the entire school year attempting to involve sleepy students during a first block class. The rotating block does require students to keep up with a slightly more complicated schedule.

### ADVANTAGES OF THE ACCELERATED BLOCK

Perhaps the most obvious advantage of the accelerated block is that students and teachers alike have fewer courses at any given time. Students have a maximum of four core courses, and teachers usually teach no more than three courses per semester. Teachers' instruction and students' study are less fragmented. With longer class periods, teachers are able to utilize instructional strategies such as simulations, and short field trips, typically unmanageable with shorter class periods. With passing periods reduced by nearly half, there are fewer opportunities for hallway altercations (Queen & Isenhour, 1998).

Other advantages of the accelerated block include the opportunity for students to repeat courses without falling further behind and to take more classes in the same time frame than is possible in a traditional schedule. Because courses such as English and American History are offered during each term, not every student will take these courses at the same time as in a traditional schedule. Therefore, fewer textbooks will need to be purchased. There is also research to suggest that attendance is improved for students, and failure rates drop (Lybbert, 1998).

The 4 x 4 block also reduces the number of students a teacher sees each day. In a traditional schedule, each teacher is responsible for 150 to 175 students each day. When teaching three classes daily on the 4 x 4 schedule, the student load is reduced by approximately 50%. Also, students have fewer teachers and fewer sets of classroom rules and routines to learn.

Lastly, the 4 x 4 block offers the advantage of two fresh starts per year. This is especially helpful in maintaining the momentum of learning during the long period between winter break and spring vacation. This second *first day of school* also provides a fresh start for teachers and students.

## DISADVANTAGES OF THE ACCELERATED BLOCK

### SEQUENCING COURSES

The most widely discussed disadvantage of the accelerated block is the possible retention problem due to the discontinuity that can exist between sequential courses in areas such as mathematics and foreign languages. Consequently, professionals in these areas have been among the most vocal in expressing concerns. In the 4 x 4 system, it is very possible for a student to complete Algebra I or Spanish I in December of his/her freshman year and not begin Algebra II or Spanish II until spring of the sophomore year. In some schools, geometry is sequenced after Algebra I and before Algebra II. This pattern, coupled with a 4 x 4 schedule, could result in a two-year hiatus from algebra instruction.

## ADVANCED PLACEMENT PROGRAM

Teachers of advanced placement (AP) courses also have some cause for concern. Most AP examinations are administered during the first two weeks of May. If the corresponding advanced placement course is only offered in the fall, the additional burden of review may become required of both students and teachers. Scheduling all AP courses in the spring might not be the answer either. Schools that offer several AP courses could encounter further difficulty in that enrollment in one AP course might preclude students from enrolling in another due to scheduling conflicts.

## FINE ARTS AND ATHLETICS

Certain programs, such as fine arts and vocational/agriculture, need to meet all year due to outside obligations such as concerts, livestock shows, and contests. In addition, newspaper and yearbook classes need to meet all year to facilitate complete coverage of school activities for their publications. Athletic programs also find themselves in the same quandary. Students who participate in more than one sport may need to enroll in athletics all year. Those who participate in more than one extracurricular activity are in an even tighter squeeze. It is possible that a student who both sings in the choir and participates in a sport could graduate from high school with half of her/his credits in athletics and music. While both programs are important to any school culture, it is simple to see the difficulty created when the students affected also look to schedule advanced science, mathematics, or foreign language classes.

## TRANSFER STUDENTS

Provision needs to be made for transfer students who enroll in the middle of the year. Difficulties occur when students transfer from schools that use traditional or incompatible block schedules. A student who transfers in November from a traditional school is less than halfway through coursework; the student who attends a 4 x 4 school is almost through with four courses at that same point in the school year. Looking at this issue from the opposite perspective raises this question: How do teachers help these students catch up without compromising the education of the other students? This issue is deceptively complex. Its answer is dependent on the schedule from which the student comes, the courses in which she/he is enrolled, the placement of courses in the schedule of the receiving school, and exactly how far into the current school year or term the transfer takes place.

## THE ALTERNATING BLOCK

In an *alternating* block, also called *A/B block*, students and teachers meet every other day throughout the school year. Students are usually enrolled in eight class periods; teachers normally teach six classes. As in the 4 x 4 block, classes in the alternating block vary from 70 to 90 minutes or more. An alternating block schedule is presented in Figure 2.4.

### FIGURE 2.4. STUDENT SCHEDULE IN THE ALTERNATING BLOCK

|  | "A" Day | "B" Day |
|---|---|---|
| *Block 1* | Algebra I | Vocational Agriculture I |
| *Block 2* | English I | World History |
| *Block 3* | Computer Science I | Art I |
| *Block 4* | German I | Biology I |

There are several variations in the pattern in which this two-day cycle occurs. In some schools, the cycle repeats itself with no alteration or adjustment. In others, every Monday and Wednesday are *A* days, Tuesday and Thursday are *B* days, and Fridays *alternate*. Still others assign all odd days (e.g., February 1) as *A* days and all even days (e.g., February 2) as *B* days.

### ADVANTAGES OF THE ALTERNATING BLOCK

The alternating block offers several of the same advantages as the accelerated block: opportunity to plan and to implement extended lessons, fewer passing periods, opportunity to utilize varied teaching strategies, and increased instructional time. In addition, the alternating block provides opportunity for courses to meet all year when needed. For students, homework is rarely due the next day.

Itinerant teachers may also benefit from the alternating block. For example, a teacher working in two different buildings could be assigned to one school on *A* days and a second school on *B* days, avoiding the need to race between campuses during the school day.

### DISADVANTAGES OF THE ALTERNATING BLOCK

As with any schedule, there are potential pitfalls. Especially early in the school year, students and teachers can sometimes be unsure: "Is today *A* day or *B* day?" The alternating block creates new continuity issues. Only on rare occasions do students and teachers see each other on consecutive days. In some situations, teachers might go an entire week or more without seeing a class. For students, the alternating block allows little opportunity for acceleration of coursework when desired or repetition of courses when needed (Hottenstein, 1998).

Another weakness of the alternating block is, as on a traditional schedule, students have six to eight teachers all year. This translates into six to eight subjects and six to eight sets of classroom policies and routines to learn.

### THE COPERNICAN PLAN

The Copernican Plan, developed in the 1960s by J. M. Carroll, has two main configurations, each combining blocks of differing lengths during the school day to accommodate a variety of instructional strategies. In the first configuration, students enroll in one four-hour "macroclass" each day. Macroclasses occupy the largest single time blocks in a Copernican system, and are reserved for *core* subjects such as mathematics and English. In addition, each student is also enrolled in two or three shorter seminar classes, each 70 to 90 minutes in length. Each student receives a new schedule every 30 days (Carroll, 1990).

Under the second configuration, each student is enrolled in two classes lasting two hours each. Students receive new schedules every 60 days. Activities and athletics are conducted after school under both configurations. Figures 2.5 and 2.6 depict typical student schedules using the Copernican Plan. (Figures 2.5 and 2.6 are adapted from Carroll, J. M. (1990). The Copernican Plan: Restructuring the American high school. *Phi Delta Kappan, 71*(5), 358–365.)

### FIGURE 2.5. STUDENT SCHEDULE ON THE COPERNICAN PLAN: CONFIGURATION 1

|  | *Term 1* | *Term 2* | *Term 3* | *Term 4* | *Term 5* | *Term 6* |
|---|---|---|---|---|---|---|
| *Macro-class 240 minutes* | English | US History | Alge-bra I | Biology I | Com-puter Science | Alge-bra II |
| *30–35 minutes* | Lunch | | | | | |
| *Seminar I 70 minutes* | Music | | | | | |
| *Seminar II 70 minutes* | P. E. | | | | | |
| *Seminar III 70 minutes* | Independent Research | | | | | |
| *After School* | Athletics & Activities | | | | | |

## FIGURE 2.6. STUDENT SCHEDULE ON THE
## COPERNICAN PLAN: CONFIGURATION 2

|  | *Term 1* | *Term 2* | *Term 3* |
|---|---|---|---|
| *Macroclass I* 120 *minutes* | English I | Algebra I | Computer Science |
| *Macroclass II* 120 *minutes* | US History | Biology I | Algebra II |
| 35 *minutes* | Lunch | | |
| *Seminar I* 70 *minutes* | Music | | |
| *Seminar II* 70 *minutes* | P. E. | | |
| *Seminar III* 70 *minutes* | Independent Research | | |
| *After School* | Athletics & Activities | | |

### ADVANTAGES OF THE COPERNICAN PLAN

The Copernican Plan offers teachers and students unique advantages. First, students and teachers are able to concentrate on a smaller number of classes at one time. This concentrated learning environment provides opportunity for students to spend large blocks of time with complex issues that are relevant to what is being studied in class. Interdisciplinary units are particularly well suited for the Copernican Plan. For example, a history teacher might plan a unit about the assassination of President John F. Kennedy centered on a mock trial. Mathematics and science students could study bullet trajectories and medical evidence to act as expert witnesses, debate students might act as legal counsel, and journalism students might be the press corps.

According to Carroll (1990), the most important advantage of the Copernican Plan is the limited number of students and classes for which teachers are responsible. In schools using configuration 1, teachers might teach a macroclass and one seminar. This translates to two classes and a total of 50 to 55 students instead of the 150 to 175 that teachers on traditional schedules are required to teach.

As in the alternating block, provision is made for courses that need to meet all year long. Other advantages include the opportunity for students to complete more classes, including advanced science, mathematics, and foreign language courses, and to repeat courses when necessary.

### DISADVANTAGES OF THE COPERNICAN PLAN

As with other forms of block scheduling, retention is a concern with the Copernican Plan. If a student studies Algebra I during the first 30-day macroclass of his/her freshman year, and studies Algebra II during the last macroclass of his/her sophomore year, the hiatus between math classes can be more than a calendar year. Issues such as keeping students on task for extended periods of time and difficulty placing transfers from other schools during the year are still present. For further information on models of block scheduling, the reader is urged to consult the suggested readings at the end of the chapter.

## TEACHING IN THE BLOCK:
## NEW METHODS FOR CONSTRUCTING LEARNING

Anyone who grew up in the late 1950s or early 1960s should remember Miss Landers. This remarkable woman had the daunting responsibility of shaping the intellect of the nation's most famous preadolescent, Theodore "Beaver" Cleaver. The classroom of *Leave it to Beaver* was typical for its day. Students sat in orderly rows and addressed the teacher only when the teacher first addressed them. The lessons were compartmentalized: arithmetic never mixed with science, language arts, or social studies. Learning was demonstrated through rote memory. From all appearances, Miss Landers was the only teacher in the building.

Since the premiere of *Leave it to Beaver* on October 4, 1957 (coincidentally, the same day of the Soviet launch of Sputnik I), men have walked on the moon, personal computers have replaced typewriters, and satellites have made instantaneous global communication possible. Unfortunately, most public school classrooms have not kept the same pace. In many instances, instruction is still teacher centered, lessons are still compartmentalized, learning is still demonstrated through rote memory, and teachers still yearn for opportunities to talk with each other.

The move to a block schedule is more than just a matter of restructuring time. To enact a revolution in learning, there needs to be a corresponding revolution in teaching. Instruction needs to become student centered, planning needs to be collaborative, and assessment needs to become authentic for all learners. A basic paradigm shift is needed.

## THE TEACHER-CENTERED PARADIGM: WHY IT NO LONGER WORKS

Jensen (1998) identifies three models of the teacher-centered paradigm: the apprenticeship model, the "conveyor-belt" curriculum, and behaviorism (pp. 1–2). In the apprenticeship model, the education process was embedded in the business community. To learn a trade, one sought the advice and mentorship of someone practicing that trade. The influence of the system crossed the boundaries of social class and economic status.

In the conveyor-belt curriculum, ushered in by the Industrial Revolution, education assumed a distinct identity for the first time. Students were gathered together in one place for the purpose of learning. The curriculum became standardized: everyone studied literature, mathematics, and history, for example. The conveyor-belt model emphasized the importance of "obedience, orderliness, unity, and respect for authority" (Jensen, 1998, p. 2).

The behaviorism model emerged during the 1950s and 1960s and was characterized by the belief that if a student's behavior could be properly controlled, learning would occur. Championed by B. F. Skinner and John Watson, this model reflected what was known about the brain at that time (Jensen, 1998).

Recent brain research casts new light on the education paradigm portrayed in *Leave it to Beaver*. No longer can we assume that any one instructional strategy is sufficient to reach *all* learners *all* of the time.

## THE HUMAN BRAIN: CULTIVATING THE POTENTIAL FOR LEARNING

Dendrites are the receptive surfaces of neurons that make possible the construction of knowledge in the human brain. Neurons *talk* to each other through chemicals, called neurotransmitters, that flow from cell to cell. Research demonstrates that the more enriched the learning environment, the more numerous and active are the neurotransmitters and dendrites (Wolfe & Brandt, 1998). The opposite is also true. Dendrites that have not been put to use die off. This process, known as pruning, takes place in impoverished learning environments (D'Arcangelo, 1998). The implication for learning is clear: the more a person is exposed to an enriched, challenging instructional environment, the more he/she will learn, because the *capacity to learn* has increased (Bruer, 1998).

---

### BUILDING BLOCK:
### BRAIN RESEARCH AND
### TEACHING IN THE BLOCK

Extended periods of time afforded by the block schedule provide an ideal forum for incorporating diverse teaching strategies. Coupled with proper pacing, diverse teaching strategies can build the enriched, challenging instructional environment called for in the latest brain research.

---

To cultivate an enriched learning environment, Wolfe and Brandt (1998) indicate that, "We educators are either growing dendrites or letting them wither and die. The trick is to determine what constitutes an enriched environment" (p. 11). Additional brain research findings, according to Wolfe and Brandt (1998), include:

- The development of the brain is an integrated process. Skills are not learned one at a time, but are developed continuously;
- The brain makes meaning through exposure to an enriched environment;
- The brain is essentially curious, and it must be to survive. It constantly seeks connections between the new and the known; and,
- The brain is innately social and collaborative.... Learning is enhanced when [students have the] opportunity to discuss their thinking out loud.... (p. 11)

## BUILDING BLOCK: TEACHING AND THE HUMAN BRAIN

The use of varied teaching techniques is compatible with the brain's natural development. Cooperative learning activities assist students in making connections with concepts and with each other.

The varied teaching strategies possible within the framework of longer blocks of time can be a powerful *toolkit* for teachers to build the enriched environment needed for learning. An enriched learning environment is also a potent agent for maintaining student attention during extended class periods.

## EMOTION AND LEARNING

Another important finding about learning is the strong connection between learning and emotion. Emotional involvement is prerequisite to learning; emotion is the engine that propels attention, which, in turn, makes learning and memory possible (D'Arcangelo, 1998). The normal activity of the human brain is roughly analogous to a mountain range. The level of brain activity has peaks and valleys:

> The normal human brain works in periods of high levels of attention, followed by periods of low levels of attention. The brain needs downtime.... If you're introducing something fairly new and complex to students, they'll probably need more downtime more often than if you are reviewing material that they already know pretty well. (D'Arcangelo, 1998, pp. 24–25)

During downtime, the brain strengthens its hold on new knowledge. It is believed that memory is formed through a process called long-term potentiation, that is a strengthening of bridges across gaps between neurons called synapses (Jensen, 1998).

---

**BUILDING BLOCK:**
**DOWNTIME IS IMPORTANT**

Strategically placed downtime during extended learning periods can help increase the retention of what has been learned; hence, the need for several different types of learning activities is essential in a block schedule.

---

## INTELLIGENCE

(The material in this section is extrapolated from H. Gardner (1993), *Frames of mind: The theory of multiple intelligences.* New York: Basic Books. We note that this seminal work was first published in 1983.)

For more than a century, intelligence has been viewed as a singular entity. Howard Gardner challenged this belief in his landmark work *Frames of Mind: The Theory of Multiple Intelligences.* Gardner offers the following list of criteria for identifying capacities as intelligences: an identifiable core, a characteristic pattern of development, a number of specific end-states, neurological representation, and discernible patterns of breakdown (1993, p. 242). Using this list, Gardner proposes the existence of seven distinct intelligences.

## VERBAL/LINGUISTIC INTELLIGENCE

According to Gardner, poetry best illustrates verbal/linguistic intelligence. Three domains of language are identified: semantics, phonology, and syntax. Semantics refers to the examination of the meanings of words, phonology describes the sounds or musical quality of words, and syntax is a collective term for the rules that govern the order of words and their inflections. In Gardner's view, language performs four major functions: rhetorical (to convince), mnemonic (to remember), explanatory (to explain), and metalinguistic (to reflect upon language itself). Verbal/linguistic intelligence is primarily vocal, not written.

## MUSICAL/RHYTHMIC INTELLIGENCE

The core components of musical intelligence are pitch, rhythm, and timbre. Pitch defines the auditory frequency at which sound occurs. Rhythm defines the relationship of a series of pitches over the continuum of time, and timbre, the qualities of a given tone. Musical intelligence, according to Gardner, is the earliest of the intelligences to emerge and is closely linked to emotion.

Music has its own syntax from which a composer is able to build musical compositions. Persons with high levels of musical intelligence are able to discern patterns such as scales and arpeggios that can be deeply embedded in composition. Through commonalties such as ratios and patterns, musical intelligence is closely related to logical/mathematical intelligence.

## LOGICAL/MATHEMATICAL INTELLIGENCE

Logical/mathematical intelligence is the first intelligence identified by Gardner that is not auditory in nature. It is built on a platform of quantity and sequence. Early recognition of logical/mathematical intelligence can be manifested in the ability to collect and quantify groups of objects into sets. The highest level of logical/mathematical intelligence is the ability to transfer concrete operations such as counting to abstract problem solving. This, according to Gardner, is the essence of higher mathematics. The most central gift within logical/mathematical intelligence is the ability to skillfully manipulate long chains of reasoning.

## VISUAL/SPATIAL INTELLIGENCE

Gardner describes visual/spatial intelligence as the ability:

> ...To perceive the visual world accurately, to perform transformations and modifications upon one's initial perceptions, and to be able to re-create aspects of one's visual experience, even in the absence of relevant physical stimuli. (Gardner, 1993, p. 173)

Visual/spatial intelligence is manifested in activities such as problem solving, the visual arts, and games such as chess. The anticipation of future moves depends on a special type of visual memory.

## BODILY/KINESTHETIC INTELLIGENCE

Bodily/kinesthetic intelligence is, perhaps, best demonstrated by the art of mimes. All communication with the mime's audience is dependent on physical motion. Another mature form of bodily/kinesthetic intelligence is dance. Bodily/kinesthetic intelligence has two components: movement of the body itself and the manipulation of objects.

## INTERPERSONAL INTELLIGENCE

Interpersonal intelligence is the ability to discern different feelings, motivations, and temperaments in other people. Levels of this intelligence range from a small child discerning basic differences in people to adults reading the intentions of other people. Examples of interpersonal intelligence abound: a salesperson closing a deal, a politician soliciting support for a project, and a teacher speaking with parents.

### *INTRAPERSONAL INTELLIGENCE*

Intrapersonal intelligence is the ability to discern one's own feelings. At its most basic level, intrapersonal intelligence is the ability that allows a person to withdraw one's hand from a hot burner. At is highest level, this ability is revealed through introspective writers and therapists who help others discern difference in highly complex sets of feelings.

Gardner refers to the intrapersonal and interpersonal intelligences as personal intelligences. The personal intelligences are different from other intelligences in that these types of intelligences are:

- Difficult to track;
- Firmly linked to each other;
- Easily misdiagnosed;
- More strongly rewarded; and,
- Encouraged more often.

### *NATURALISTIC INTELLIGENCE*

A few years later, Gardner added an eighth intelligence, naturalistic intelligence. Naturalistic intelligence is man's ability to perceive differences in living things and to interpret and extrapolate meaning from other features of the natural world such as rock formations, waterfalls, and clouds. This intelligence is beneficial in such diverse endeavors as landscape architecture, weather forecasting, and hunting.

## IMPLICATIONS FOR THE BLOCK: CHANGING TEACHING

In light of recent brain research and the complex nature of human intelligence, the need for enriched, varied instruction is clear, regardless of which type of schedule is being used. To facilitate growth in diverse learners, teaching needs to be diverse. No single instructional methodology can stimulate all human perceptions all of the time. Additionally, the needs of specific learners change *within class periods*. Specifically, teachers in the block need to:

+ Implement diverse teaching strategies;
+ Facilitate student-directed learning; and,
+ Weave technology into the fabric of their teaching.

## DIVERSE TEACHING STRATEGIES

Walker (1998) indicates that less than 30% of students learn by lecture and, after about 15 minutes, their attention begins to evaporate. This limited attention span, coupled with the need for an enriched learning environment as demonstrated by current brain research, completes a convincing case for utilizing diverse teaching strategies. Strategies particularly useful during block class periods include Socratic seminars, cooperative learning, simulations, learning centers, presentations, multimedia, and lecture (Canady & Rettig, 1996; Marshak, 1997).

Class periods involving diverse teaching strategies require more planning than simply lecturing. In addition to planning multiple learning activities, teachers also need to plan the *segues* (transitions) to get students from one activity to the next. To facilitate planning these more complex class periods, Canady and Rettig (1996) suggest dividing class periods into segments. Dividing class periods into segments helps the teacher determine how long each learning activity should be and the best way of transitioning between learning activities.

## STUDENT-DIRECTED LEARNING

Learning needs to become more student-centered instead of teacher-centered. Teachers need to become the *guide on the side* instead of the *sage on the stage*. This belief is echoed in the constructivist literature. Dewey (1938) stated: "There is no point in the philosophy of progressive education which is sounder than its emphasis upon the importance of the participation of the learner in the formation of purposes which direct his activities in the learning process" (p. 67). O'Neil (1998) echoes the need for student-centered learning: "People learn by actively constructing knowledge..." (p. 51).

## WEAVING TECHNOLOGY INTO THE FABRIC OF TEACHING

The infusion of technology into America's classrooms serves two key purposes. First, technology can assist in moving learning from theory to practice. Through technology, history students can apply lessons from the past and not merely recite them. Science and mathematics students can apply problem-solving skills to real-world problems and not just to notebook paper. Computers can assist in keeping even the most disinterested learners engaged. In addition, the Internet may be the most complete library in the world. It can facilitate access to persons and places all over the world.

The second purpose of technology in the classroom is to prepare students to function in a technologically advanced world. As the twenty-first century dawns, virtually every employer uses computers: attorneys produce legal documents such as wills, restaurants track food and labor costs, hotels record guest reservations, architects draw building plans, and sanitation workers design collection routes.

## SUMMARY

A fundamental change in the paradigm under which public education has operated for over a century needs to take place. A paradigm of collaboration and innovation is needed in planning, implementing, and assessing instruction. Fullan (1993) believes that:

> There is a ceiling effect on how much we can learn if we keep to ourselves. The ability to collaborate—on both a small and large scale—is becoming one of the core requisites of postmodern society. People need one another to learn and to accomplish things. (p. 17)

If teachers are to be successful within a block schedule, they first need to be successful learners themselves. Schools need to be synonymous with learning organizations. The energy that is created through collaboration becomes *synergy*. Zepeda (1999a) writes, "Through collaborative efforts, a community of learners creates synergy, a synchronized energy where the power of the group is more profound than any one individual" (p. 58).

The paradigm of collaboration begins when traditional hierarchies are flattened. Supervisors and teachers become *colleagues* in the deepest sense of the word. Barnett, McKowen, and Bloom (1998) indicate, "The 'us versus them' dynamic doesn't materialize, because there's no them—just us" (p. 49). It takes an *us* attitude for schools to be successful learning organizations. The *us* attitude must begin with the influence of the principal.

## SUGGESTED READINGS

Canady, R. L., & Rettig, M. D. (1995). *Block scheduling: A catalyst for change in high schools.* Larchmont, NY: Eye on Education.

Carroll, J. M. (1990). The Copernican Plan: Restructuring the American high school. *Phi Delta Kappan, 71*(5), 358–365.

Gardner, H. (1993). *Frames of mind: The theory of multiple intelligences.* New York: Basic Books.

Jensen, E. (1998). *Teaching with the brain in mind.* Alexandria, VA: Association for Supervision and Curriculum.

# 3

# THE ADMINISTRATIVE TEAM

## CHAPTER OBJECTIVES

- Examine existing supervisory and staff development roles assumed by the members of the administrative team.
- Lead the administrative team in examining their core beliefs about professional development and in developing a collective vision for adult learning in the block.
- Examine implications for practice.

There will be many changes associated with implementing a block schedule regardless of the school's context. In fact, it is the school's context that will provide the foundation for changes —for both the structure of the school itself and for the people who will be changing the way "things are done." Members of the administrative team, like the teachers manning the classrooms, will also need to examine their practices—supervisory and staff development—as well. Suggested supervisory and staff development strategies to complement the block are discussed in other chapters.

This chapter examines the administrative structures in the school and how these structures can evolve to better fit the needs of the organization. The "fit" of the changes needed in the structure of the administrative team and the examination of the work that these professionals do is paramount if success is to be assured. Without such an examination of administrative practices, the human resources of the school's administrative team will not be synchronized to work at providing for the needs of teachers as they work at changing their practices to maximize the time afforded by the block schedule. The organization cannot systemically change for the better unless all other significant structures within the school change in like fashion. Logic tells us this.

The members of the administrative team will need to examine their current instructional leadership practices in relation to the new needs of the school. Although the principal is charged with providing the conditions necessary to promote ongoing support for change and professional development once the block schedule has been implemented, there are others on the administrative team who also need to examine their current instructional leadership practices. This examination should signal to the principal that administrative team members need learning opportunities to attend to their professional development as well. It would be counterproductive for the members of the administrative team to be excluded from enhancing their supervisory skills.

The type of collaboration explored in this book cannot exist in a school unless it is consistently modeled by the administrative team (e.g., associate principal, assistant principals, department chairs, instructional deans, lead teachers, and grade-level coordinators). The principal's efforts need to focus on finding the time and human resources necessary to promote the development of the leadership team. The administrative team needs to learn how to work together in order to:

♦ Build a unified vision for supervision and professional development in the block;

♦ Serve as valuable resources to teachers;

♦ Grow as professionals from their work in the school;

♦ Forward the needs of teachers to the forefront; and,

♦ Coordinate and provide appropriate learning opportunities based on these needs.

To achieve these goals, the principal needs to purposefully cast the net to include others in the instructional leadership of the school. With the involvement of administrative team members working under the same set of assumptions and values about teachers and their growth, there can be a more powerful message sent to teachers—support—through a more unified and coordinated program for professional development. Team members, if they are not on the "same page," will send "mixed messages" to teachers about the importance and value of professional growth. Credibility will diminish in the eyes of teachers who will be looking for support and assistance as they examine and modify the instructional practices utilized to teach in the block.

## EXAMINING THE ADMINISTRATIVE TEAM STRUCTURE

Although there are differences in the composition of administrative and supervisory personnel at the high school level, most systems utilize assistant principals and department chairs. Depending on the school's size and location (e.g., urban, suburban, or rural), additional positions such as an associate principal or an instructional dean might round out the administrative team. The people who fill these positions have varying involvement with the instructional program. With the change to the block schedule, the principal is in an excellent position to examine the pool of supervisory personnel and to work at building new instructional roles with these professionals.

## WHY EXPLORE THE ADMINISTRATIVE TEAM COMPOSITION

The principal cannot possibly meet the challenge of providing resources *without the assistance of others*. Leadership needs to come from the entire community, working collaboratively to improve teaching and learning. With the move to a block schedule, there are numerous implications for the members of the administrative team. Administrative team members, like teachers, will need to regulate their schedules. One consideration is the availability of time to conduct classroom observation as displayed in Figure 3.1.

**FIGURE 3.1. CLASS PERIOD AVAILABILITY FOR CLASSROOM OBSERVATIONS IN A TRADITIONAL SCHEDULE**

| Daily Periods | Days Per Semester | Total Available Class Periods to Conduct Classroom Observations |
|:---:|:---:|:---:|
| 6 | 90 | 540 |
| 7 | 90 | 630 |

In stark contrast, Figure 3.2 examines the availability of class time in different block schedule configurations.

## FIGURE 3.2. CLASS PERIOD AVAILABILITY FOR CLASSROOM OBSERVATIONS IN THE BLOCK SCHEDULE

| Block Type | Periods/ Days | Days/ Term | Total Available Class Periods |
|---|---|---|---|
| 4 x 4/Alternating Block | 4 | 90 | 360 |
| Trimester | 3 | 60 | 180 |
| Copernican: | | | |
|    4-Hour Macroclass | 1 | 30 | 30 Periods Per Term |
|    2-Hour Macroclass | 2 | 60 | 60 Periods Per Term |

Just as teachers moving to the block schedule must be aware of pacing, so too must supervisors. When class periods are lengthened, the number of class periods available for classroom observations decreases. Figure 3.2 illustrates the magnitude to which the number of available periods decreases when a block schedule is implemented. For example, a school with a 6-period day that adopts a 4 x 4 or an alternating block reduces the number of class periods for observation by 33 percent (540 class periods to 360). If this same school was operating on a 7-period day, the number of available class periods is reduced by 43 percent!

When combined with the need for extended observations in the block schedule (Zepeda, 1999b), the principal faces a dilemma: Teachers still need to be supervised and, in the block schedule, the need for extended classroom observations is critical, but the number of opportunities for classroom observations is drastically reduced. This reduction in available class periods might be a "blessing in disguise," however, in that the days of waiting to visit classrooms two or three days before annual evaluations are due, are now over. This is a sigh of relief as the intent of supervision is to provide ongoing and systematic growth opportunities for teachers.

The solutions to this dilemma are complex because supervision and staff development will need to be reinvented to accommodate the changes in schedules. Reinventing supervision cannot be accomplished unless the principal purposefully engages the entire administrative team in this process, while getting feedback on what makes sense and is needed by teachers to promote learning.

## EXPLORE THE ADMINISTRATIVE TEAM COMPOSITION

### ASSISTANT PRINCIPALS

Time and demands will change for principals as they move toward implementing a block schedule. It is not uncommon for principals to assume that they bear the weight of being *the* instructional leader and that assistant principals assist by fulfill such tasks as managing discipline, athletics, facilities, and activities. Although these critical tasks are deserving of attention, assistant principals typically have a "narrow" job description that *restricts* them from emerging as instructional leaders. Most assistant principals, according to Marshall (1992), "can be an instructional leader in rare instances....Quite possibly, the duties of assistant principals stop them from developing as instructional leaders" (pp. 14–15). When assistant principals become overidentified as gatekeepers and managers of non-instructional areas, boundaries are created. Unfortunately, teachers, who do not have an affiliation with these areas, find little reason to interact with assistant principals.

Because of the frenetic work world of the assistant principal, who assumes multiple duties and responsibilities, there is traditionally little "built-in" time for learning about and then assuming a stronger instructional leadership position or status within the school. To assist the principal in examining the responsibilities of the assistant principals, Figure 3.3 is provided. Note the column, *Area of Interest,* in this figure. Although the assistant principal might not currently be involved in this interest, it is important for the principal to begin thinking of ways to link interests with building level needs created as a result of moving toward the block schedule.

---

### FIGURE 3.3. ASSISTANT PRINCIPAL PROFILE

---

| Position/<br>Person | Responsible For | Areas of<br>Interest |
|---|---|---|
| A.P. Beck | English and Foreign Language Department Activities; Parent/Teacher Conferences; Counseling Department; Certified Support Staff (social worker, psychologist, school nurse); Special Education; Non-certified Staff; Library Media Center; and Discipline (A through H) | Mentoring and Induction |
| A.P. Callahan | Social Studies and P.E. Departments; Athletics and Intramurals; Bussing; Staff Development; Community and Public Relations; Service Learning; and Discipline (I through P) | Peer Coaching |
| A.P. Thomas | Science and Business Departments; Fine Arts; Field Trips; School-to-Work Program; Homecoming; Student Photos; Jr./Sr. Prom; and Discipline (Q through Z) | Study Groups |
| A.P. Werner | Mathematics Department; In-School Suspension; Faculty Attendance; Technology; Awards Assemblies; Federal Programs (Chapter, Free & Reduced Lunch Program, At-Risk); Facilities; Police Department Liaison; and Safety Committee | Videotape Analysis |

What can the principal learn from such a profile? The information in Figure 3.3 shows that the assistant principals have interests in mentoring, induction, peer coaching, staff development, study groups, and videotape analysis of teaching. Just because an assistant principal has an interest in a topic, does not mean that he/she has expertise, knowledge, and training to design a program. Nor does this interest (with or without expertise) necessarily mean that the assistant principal has the time during the course of the day to work within this area of interest.

## DEPARTMENT CHAIRS

Although there are no universals about the work of department chairs, these professionals have the ability to exert a great deal of influence over the curriculum and interact more often with teachers than do principals and assistant principals. Department chairs are in a unique position because they:

♦ Come more immediately from the rank and file of teaching;

♦ Continue to teach as they fulfill departmental responsibilities;

♦ Maintain office space in the departmental office or away from the main office; and,

♦ Are identified as experts in the overall curriculum and its sequence, content areas, grade-level initiatives, and instruction.

In some states, department chairs are certified administrators who are involved in the formal supervision and evaluation of teachers in addition to coordinating the curriculum in a designated area (e.g., math, English, social studies, science, fine arts, and business) and myriad other duties. Often, these chairs carry reduced teaching loads based on the size of the department and the amount of supervisory duty assigned.

In other states, department chairs have no formal supervisory responsibility and are not certified as such, but they are involved in working with teachers in more informal ways (e.g., mentoring new teachers and peer coaching), and formally coordinating curriculum development, textbook adoption, and resource allocation within the department. Unfortunately, release time is rarely built into the daily schedule. Departmental responsibilities are fulfilled either during planning time, before and after school, or when necessary, release time is provided during the day. Figure 3.4 provides a profile of department chairs, noting their areas of interest.

---

**FIGURE 3.4. DEPARTMENT CHAIR PROFILE**

---

| Department | Chair | Release Time | Areas of Interest |
|---|---|---|---|
| English | Klein | 4 Periods | Action Research |
| Social Studies | Smith | 2 Periods | Unknown |
| Mathematics | van Deming | 4 Periods | Study Groups |
| Special Education | Spears | 3 Periods | Action Research |
| Foreign Language | Hernandez | 2 Periods | Cooperative Learning |
| Business | Josten | 1 Period | Study Groups |
| Fine Arts | Franklin | 3 Periods | Multiple Intelligences |
| Science | Gibbons | 4 Periods | Mentoring, Induction, First-year Teachers |
| Guidance/ Counseling | Merit | Reduced Student Assignment | Study Groups, Mentoring |

---

From the information provided in Figure 3.4, the principal discovers that many of the department chairs have similar interests (e.g., action research, study groups, and mentoring) that parallel those of the assistant principals. The profile also illustrates that some department chairs have more release time than others. Release time contingent on the number of faculty in the department will need to be examined in light of the block schedule adopted by the school. The same caveat made in the profile of the assistant principals is made here as well: interest does not guarantee expertise or time in the daily schedule to put interests to action.

The question for the principal to ponder is, "Can the department chairs' position be expanded to provide more formalized and ongoing support utilizing such processes as coaching, mentoring, action research, and study groups?" The answer resides in the context of the school. Here are some areas to consider before answering this question:

◆ How much release time is afforded to each chair? How is release time determined?

◆ What responsibilities do the department chairs assume?

◆ Are department chairs classified as administrators? Do chairs formally supervise and evaluate teachers?

◆ With the change to the block schedule, will release periods increase? Decrease?

◆ Do the department chairs and assistant principals coordinate efforts (e.g., supervision, evaluation, and staff development)?

◆ How can the efforts of the assistant principals, department chairs, and grade level coordinators be better coordinated?

◆ Can the school system support releasing all department chairs from the same amount of teaching? Would such a change create dissatisfaction among department chairs who oversee "supersize" departments?

◆ Are department chairs afforded the opportunity to attend staff development activities (e.g., conferences and workshops) that address their own learning needs in regard to leadership skill development?

♦ Do department chairs have a forum for sharing what they have learned about leadership or other interests pursued as staff development?

♦ Are department chairs regularly included in weekly administrative meetings? Do department chairs meet frequently as a group?

By answering these questions (and perhaps others generated by the reader), the principal will be in a better position to determine if, indeed, the role of the department chair can be expanded.

## INSTRUCTIONAL DEANS, LEAD TEACHERS, AND GRADE-LEVEL COORDINATORS

Some school systems have developed new roles for teachers by creating positions such as instructional deans, lead teachers, and grade-level coordinators. These people also provide instructional and curricular support. There are no universals to what these people do because each school system is context-specific; however, there are some commonalities.

An instructional dean is a designated supervision and staff development coordinator for an entire building. The instructional dean works alongside the administration in planning and developing learning opportunities for the school. The position of instructional dean is a new and emerging one that has great promise *if configured to exclude teacher evaluation.* An instructional dean typically:

♦ Conducts formative supervision and does not evaluate teachers at the end of the year;

♦ Compiles and reports the needs of the faculty to the administration;

♦ Secures resources for teachers such as available staff development opportunities;

♦ Works with the administration to develop induction activities for new teachers; and,

♦ Provides for the development of unique and emerging programs for professional growth (e.g., peer coaching, mentoring, and inter-and intra- departmental classroom observations).

Like the instructional dean, lead teachers and grade-level coordinators also work with teachers. A lead teacher is usually released for a portion of the day to work with fellow teachers on instructional and curricular matters. The lead teacher and grade-level coordinators do not formally observe teachers unless the observations are part of an informal peer coaching or mentoring program.

Grade-level coordinators are more likely to have a spot in larger high schools that have up to twenty people in a single department (e.g., English). A grade level coordinator works primarily alongside the department chair, but coordinates a relatively small slice of the curriculum. For example, a freshman English grade-level coordinator typically:

♦ Oversees the curriculum at the freshman level;

♦ Conducts meetings among freshman English teachers on a regular basis;

♦ Coordinates with the department chair on the textbook adoption process, the development of the schoolwide freshman English district and/or building-level curriculum guides, and other curricular activities;

♦ Identifies with grade-level teachers the areas of the curriculum that need attention;

♦ Targets specific areas of staff development that are needed to meet grade-level goals and objectives;

♦ Communicates with other grade-level coordinators to work on such activities as the alignment of the curriculum from one grade level to another;

♦ Communicates the needs of the grade level to the department chair; and,

♦ Shares information about developments in the field with members of the grade-level.

Although the proceeding sections provided a thumbnail sketch of the roles that members of the administrative team typically assume at the high school level, more information that is context-specific is needed. The principal needs to assess what human resources are available, what types of skills these people bring to the setting, what types of skills need to be developed more fully in these people, what policies dictate the duties these people are able to "legally" fulfill, and, more importantly, what resources of the administrative team can be better deployed so that teachers can benefit from these resources? These are tough questions to answer. The answers will contain the information needed to maximize the interests and talents of administrative team members. The maxim, *Know Your People*, needs to guide the principal in focusing the overall efforts of the administrative team.

## "KNOW YOUR PEOPLE" BY DEVELOPING A PROFILE OF THE ADMINISTRATIVE TEAM

To begin the process of assessing the strengths of the administrative team and to better match the individual strengths to instructional and curricular areas, the principal is encouraged to develop a profile of the administrative team and other support personnel utilized in the building. Figure 3.5 on page 76 is a sample of the human resources of a high school.

Although the information presented so far can profile the people who comprise the leadership team, another step in the process is needed: What programs to support teachers are in place? Figure 3.6 on page 77 provides a view of what programs are in place at Happy High School.

## NEW SUPERVISORY ROLES FOR THE ADMINISTRATIVE TEAM

For supervision and staff development on the block to change, the principal will need to purposefully focus attention on unifying the efforts of the administrative team, regardless of the team's composition. To accomplish this goal, the principal needs to examine ways in which the work of these people can complement instructional leadership in the block. With the

## FIGURE 3.5. HUMAN RESOURCES AT HAPPY HIGH SCHOOL

| Member | Certificate to Supervise | Interests |
|---|---|---|
| Principal | Y | C, M, I, SD |
| Associate Principal Smith | Y | AR, C, SG |
| Assistant Principal 1 Crow | Y | SG, SD,M, FYTs |
| Assistant Principal 2 Davenport | Y | C, FYTs, AR |
| Assistant Principal 3 Turner | Y | AR, SD |
| Department Chairs | Y | |
| English | Y | SD, FYTs |
| Mathematics | Y | AR, C, SG |
| Social Studies | Y | M, FYTs |
| Science | Y | C, M |
| Special Education | Y | AR |
| Foreign Language | Y | I, SD |
| Business | Y | C, M |
| Guidance | Y | AR, C, SG |
| Grade-Level Coordinators | N | M, FYTs, C, M, I, SD |

LEGEND: AR = Action Research; C = Coaching; FYTs = First-Year Teachers; I = Induction; M = Mentoring; SD = Staff Development; SG = Study Group

## FIGURE 3.6. PROGRAMS IN PLACE THAT
## SUPPORT PROFESSIONAL GROWTH

| Program | Coordinator(s) | Function |
|---------|----------------|----------|
| First-Year Teacher Induction Program | Principal & A.P. | • Induct FYTs into the school's culture<br>• Help FYTs through new procedures (attendance, discipline, parent-teacher nights)<br>• Assist new teachers in developing instructional strategies<br>• Review school and district documents and policies |
| Mentor Teacher Program | A.P. | • Assist with mentoring FYTs<br>• Provide departmental assistance to FYTs<br>• Socialize teachers: school culture, norms, and values |
| Study Groups | A.P. | • Provide a forum for teachers to study a particular topic of interest |

number of changes that the block schedule will require teachers to make, teachers will need support.

The real work of examining the structure of the administrative team can only begin with an open exploration of the values and beliefs about teaching and learning within the team. By uncovering the values and beliefs of the administrative team, the principal will be in a better position to lead the team into developing a vision for professional development.

## LEAD THE ADMINISTRATIVE TEAM IN EXAMINING THEIR CORE VALUES AND DEVELOPING A COLLECTIVE VISION FOR ADULT LEARNING IN THE BLOCK

To unify the members of the administrative team, the principal needs to provide ongoing opportunities for discussion about their core beliefs about supervision, staff development, and adult learning. Before beginning this exploration, the principal can be better prepared by knowing what:

- The instructional needs of teachers are;
- Needs lay ahead in the transition to the block; and,
- Will be needed to provide ongoing support for the block once it has been implemented.

By having a "ball park" indication of these needs, the principal can better:

- Forecast the types of resources needed to meet needs in relation to the block schedule adopted;
- Ensure alignment in meeting both the needs of the system and its people;
- Match the interests of the administrative team with needs; and,
- Determine what types of staff development are needed by members of the administrative team so they can be better prepared to work in more proactive ways with teachers.

By involving the administrative team in defining their role in professional development a more unified, systematic, and coherent plan can be developed that will better utilize the strengths found within the members of the administrative team. The "talk" over time by the members of the administrative team can serve as a compass for ongoing learning for the organization.

## UNCOVER CORE VALUES AND
## BELIEFS ABOUT PROFESSIONAL GROWTH

To assist the principal, the following topical areas should be included in the initial discussions:

- What do you believe given our current situation (pre-block or implementing the block), you can contribute to adult learning needs?
- What do you believe teachers want from professional development?
- When teachers feel good about teaching, what is occurring in classrooms? Faculty meetings? Staff development sessions?
- What aspects of your current position do you think add to promoting professional growth for teachers? For yourself?
- With the changes associated with the block schedule, what types of support do you think our teachers will need? From these support needs, which ones do you feel you can provide?
- Given your current duties and responsibilities, how can you "plug in' to an interest you have in professional development and help meet a need of the school? What will get in your way? How can the team help by restructuring areas of responsibility and duty?
- What staff development do you need in order to help you assist teachers better?

As these discussions continue, the principal will be in a better position to assist the team in developing a vision for professional development in the block. By having a vision for professional development, the principal will be able to harness the talents of the administrative team.

## CREATING A VISION AMONG THE ADMINISTRATIVE TEAM

A vision is a set of beliefs, values, purposes, and goals that guide people. Conley (1996) believes that the vision is a powerful tool that acts as an *internal compass*. Sergiovanni (1994) believes that the vision helps to establish norms of behavior. Norms of behavior associated with meeting the vision are essential in that the vision "needs to be institutionalized in policies, programs, and procedures" (Starratt, 1996, p. 109).

The value of a vision is its ability to unify the needs of the people with those of the organization. The vision serves many purposes. It:

- ◆ Unifies people within the organizational structure;
- ◆ Assists with establishing a plan;
- ◆ Signals an action orientation to operationalizing the plan;
- ◆ Focuses people on the future; and,
- ◆ Promotes growth by providing the means for people to stretch as a result of facing the challenges associated with reaching for the vision.

With these purposes, it is evident that a vision can be powerful. The power is derived from the process of the work and effort people extend in developing the vision. *Developing the vision is ongoing.*

If the vision is to be taken seriously, then the vision must take a form and life of its own within the school. The vision cannot just be committed to writing and filed in a drawer; although, it would be difficult to examine changes and beliefs about supervision over time without committing the vision to writing.

A vision must be brought to life with members of the learning community involved in intensive and frequent discussion, ongoing reflection, fault-free experimentation, and constant evaluation on efforts and effects of the vision as its principles are manifested in behaviors (change in practices). Hong (1996) refers to the process of revisiting and refining the vision as "purposeful tinkering." Purposeful tinkering creates the opportunity for the vision to be constantly examined, making modifications to reach the vision, possible.

A vision about supervisory beliefs is not enough to carry the momentum for administrative team members to function in ways that will support teachers in a block schedule. First, administrative team members and support personnel need staff development to increase their potential, and second, these professionals need to learn how to work with an overriding belief that to provide for the needs of teachers, there is a need to develop "out of the box thinking" so that practices for all members of the learning community can change.

## STAFF DEVELOPMENT FOR ADMINISTRATIVE TEAM MEMBERS AND SUPPORT PERSONNEL

Staff development for the administrative team and support personnel needs to build capacity within the individual so that they can:

- ◆ Utilize instructional leadership skills;
- ◆ Be involved in activities that promote ongoing development and refinement of instructional leadership skills;
- ◆ Develop the motivation to take risks by experimenting with leadership practices and procedures within the block schedule;
- ◆ Increase professional awareness and predict in advance what types of support are needed to meet their own needs and the needs of others; and,
- ◆ Challenge their own instructional leadership practices into higher levels of performance.

## PRACTICES FOR THE BLOCK THAT CAN PROMOTE COHERENCE IN UNIFYING THE EFFORTS OF THE ADMINISTRATIVE TEAM

To build capacity in members of the administrative team and support personnel, the principal is encouraged to examine the Coherence Model (Zepeda, 1994) found in Figure 1.5 on page 29. The Coherence Model illustrates the interconnected nature of professional growth for adults by purposefully linking such activities as goal setting, multiple informal and formal observations, staff development and supervisory initiatives such as action research and coaching (both peer and cognitive), and evaluation. The power of the Coherence Model comes from the scaffolding of learning and the application of newly learned or refined information across each one of these growth-promoting processes. Coherence is also a prerequisite for unifying the efforts of the administrative team as they work with teachers in a block schedule. Changes in administrative practices can only survive if the principal, along with the members of the administrative team and support personnel, is able to:

♦ *Redefine relationships* with each other and with teachers. This redefining process begins with the principal learning, as Blase and Blase (1997) found in their research, how to "unlead" (p. 30). The hierarchical structures found within leadership teams (e.g., principal, associate principal, assistant principal, deans, instructional deans, department chairs, lead teachers, and grade level coordinators) need to be flattened.

♦ *Share responsibility for learning.* All need to assume an active role in providing learning opportunities for themselves as they work with teachers providing resources for growth.

♦ *Create an atmosphere of interdependence.* Each member of the team needs to feel a sense of belonging by being able to contribute to individual and collective learning opportunities developed working alongside, not only fellow administrative team members, but also, teachers.

♦ *Make time for professional development.* Time is often cited as the main reason why principals and other members of the administrative team cannot function as instructional leaders. Consider your reaction if a teacher indicated that he/she did not have time to make it to the B block or to correct semester exams.

♦ *Develop the administrative team plan for professional development in the block with teacher needs guiding the process.* No plan, if it is not grounded in the needs of the community and its learners, will yield significant results.

♦ *Rotate responsibilities.* Rotation of specific duties and responsibilities associated with professional development can assist in getting all members of the administrative team on the same proverbial page. This rotation can also assist with breaking down barriers between people within the organization.

♦ *Link schoolwide initiatives.* The coordination of initiatives will reduce unnecessary duplication of programs between departments or areas and allow the principal to better work at providing resources to support initiatives.

These suggestions, if implemented and frequently monitored by the members of the learning community, can create the conditions necessary to go beyond making learning the fabric or tapestry of professional growth. The organization itself will become seamless as the base of leadership multiplies.

## SUMMARY

Moving to the block necessitates steadfast action on the part of the principal to provide the conditions for members of the administrative team to grow by assuming more expanded roles as instructional leaders. Supervision and staff development will remain relatively uneventful spectator sports for administrative team members unless they are readied to assume new professional roles within the school community. This readiness begins by examining core beliefs about supervision, staff development, and adult learning. Readiness is translated into practice for administrative team members only if staff development opportunities are provided for them. The members of the administrative team must strengthen their own leadership skills if the principal expects learning to transform teaching in the block.

## SUGGESTED READINGS

Blase, J. R., & Blase, J. (1997). *The fire is back! Principals sharing school governance.* Thousand Oaks, CA: Corwin Press, Inc.

Sergiovanni, T.J. (1994). *Building community in schools.* San Francisco: Jossey-Bass.

Starratt, R. J. (1995). *Leaders with vision: The quest for school renewal.* Thousand Oaks, CA: Corwin Press, Inc.

# 4

# READYING FOR THE BLOCK: STAFF DEVELOPMENT AND SUPERVISION TO GET YOU THERE

## CHAPTER OBJECTIVES

- ◆ Identify applications of staff development models for teaching in the block.
- ◆ Outline strategies for auditing the curriculum and instruction.
- ◆ Describe initiatives that forward preparation for teaching in the block.
- ◆ Highlight teaching strategies that enhance learning in block periods.

The building of a house begins with the foundation. How the foundation is prepared is based on several factors: the land on which the house is to be built, the features to be included in the house, and the size of the house. The foundation must not only support all that comprises the house, but must *complement* the house as well. The same is true when restructuring schools. School restructuring efforts, to be successful, must be built on a firm foundation of teacher leadership, designed according to the school's context, and rooted in meeting current and future needs.

The foundation of a school is its teachers. This foundation must be ready to support and complement change initiatives. Learning is transformed only when teaching is transformed first. Darling-Hammond (1995) states:

> The importance of transforming teaching is becoming ever more clear as schools are expected to find ways to support and connect with the needs of all learners…[t]eachers must be able to develop learning experiences that accommodate a variety of cognitive styles, with activities that broaden rather than reduce the range of possibilities for learning…. (p. 155)

Even as a block schedule is being designed, staff development initiatives to prepare teachers should already be in place with teachers and administrators working toward new understandings about the effects of time on learning. Likewise, supervisory practices need to work in concert with staff development. It is when staff development and supervision are linked as complements to each other that learning for adults can be purposeful.

## A COMPREHENSIVE STAFF DEVELOPMENT PLAN FOR THE BLOCK

For teachers to be adequately prepared to implement a new initiative, they must be equipped with the proper resources. For the purposes of this chapter, resources are defined as the processes, skills, and procedures that empower teachers with the correct tools to examine their own practices in regard to curriculum, content coverage, instructional strategies, and pacing.

## STAFF DEVELOPMENT THAT MEETS VARIED LEARNING NEEDS

The varied learning needs of teachers preparing for a block schedule require a staff development plan that offers diverse learning opportunities. This challenge is most effectively met by principals who provide teachers with multiple learning opportunities. Zepeda (1999a) writes that:

> Needs are as individual as the people and organizations that possess them. Staff development designs that work for one initiative might not work well for another…. Effective principals customize staff development by mixing and matching different models… staff development can be, and…should be *purposely eclectic*…. (p. 96, emphasis supplied)

Many models can and should be an important part of a school's staff development plan. None is sufficient by itself. Staff development models that are particularly well suited for assisting teachers to prepare for a block schedule are examined in Figure 4.1. It is important to note that each model profiled in Figure 4.1 can easily be job-embedded. Each model, when properly implemented, becomes a natural part of the teacher's daily work routine. For detailed information on these staff development models, consult the suggested readings at the end of this chapter.

To assist teachers in preparing for the block, effective principals provide opportunities for teachers to:

- Audit teaching strategies they currently use;
- Modify existing teaching strategies and learn new ones;
- Experiment with varying instruction to complement new time parameters;
- Develop methods for transitioning a class from one learning activity to another; and,
- Design student assessment aligned with instruction in the block.

### FIGURE 4.1. STAFF DEVELOPMENT MODELS WITH APPLICATIONS TO BLOCK SCHEDULES

| Staff Development Model | Applications to Block Schedules |
| --- | --- |
| Individually Guided Learning | Reading professional literature on teaching in the block. |
| | Recording one's personal experience in transitioning to the block. |
| | Attending a workshop on using simulations in block teaching. |
| Problem-Based Learning (Learner-Centered) | Participating in a roundtable with teachers who have experience teaching in the block. |
| Problem-Based Learning (Problem-Centered) | Taking part in a simulation designed for probationary teachers to help them identify and overcome research-identified, first-year teacher problems within the context of the block schedule. |
| Study Groups/ Whole-School Cluster Groups | The math department studies the implementation of cooperative learning in Algebra I classes using professional literature, journals, and peer coaching. |
| | The English department, using journals and samples of student work, studies the impact of the block on teaching sentence structure. |

| *Staff Development Model* | *Applications to Block Schedules* |
|---|---|
| Action Research | The entire faculty conducts a study to determine which combinations of instructional strategies are most effective in the block from teachers' perspectives as well as from students' perspectives. |
| | The band, orchestra, and choir teachers collect and analyze data to determine how effective cooperative learning is as a structure for small group rehearsals during class. |
| Training (In-Service) | Teachers are given release time to attend workshops on classroom management in the block. |

## WHERE ARE WE NOW?

Before learning new classroom strategies, it is important for the principal to provide opportunities for teachers to inventory currently used instructional strategies. One way teachers can examine their practices in order to make informed judgments about their teaching and its relationship to curriculum, instruction, and student assessment is to conduct formal audits. Curriculum audits are data collection tools from which teachers are able to make informed decisions concerning their instructional practices. In addition, based on information gathered through audits, staff development needs, potential focus areas for classroom observations, and questions for further action research may be identified. Figure 4.2 depicts the relationship between curriculum audits, staff development, and supervision.

## FIGURE 4.2. AUDITING THE INSTRUCTIONAL PROGRAM

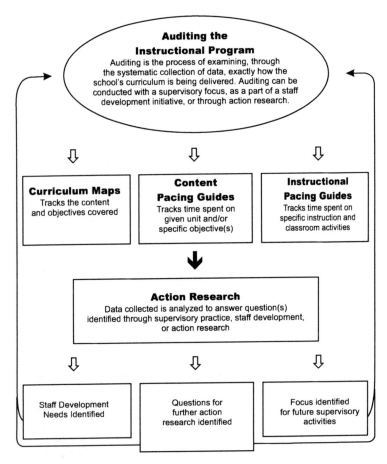

In the following pages, three types of audits (curriculum mapping, content pacing guides, and instructional pacing guides) are discussed against the backdrop of curricular and instructional practices in the block. The following strategies can be helpful in assisting teachers to audit their practices.

**BUILDING BLOCK:
AUDITING**

Auditing is the process of comparing intended instruction, objectives, and content with those actually observed or recorded in the classroom. As a result of audits, adjustments in time and instructional strategies can be made.

## CURRICULUM ANALYSIS

English (1984) identifies three curricula that exist within every school: the real curriculum, the written curriculum, and the tested curriculum. The *real curriculum* is that which is actually taught. The taught curriculum can vary from teacher to teacher within any given department. For example, if there is more than one person teaching English I or Algebra I, the taught curriculum will probably not be identical from teacher to teacher. The *written curriculum* is the official curriculum found in district or site curriculum handbooks. The *tested curriculum* is the curriculum that is assessed through standardized testing, usually mandated by the states. Figure 4.3 illustrates the curricula as described by English. We have, however, added a new dimension common to all three curricula, instruction.

The overlapping area of the curricula represents the extent to which the three curricula are aligned. The larger this area is, the more aligned a school's overall curriculum will be. Figure 4.4 depicts a highly aligned school curriculum.

The area of alignment is perhaps most worth examining. In most districts, teachers spend countless hours developing the written curriculum and constructing curriculum guides. This process usually begins with the textbook adoption process.

## FIGURE 4.3. OVERLAPPING CURRICULUM

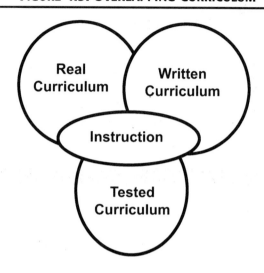

## FIGURE 4.4. A HIGHLY ALIGNED CURRICULUM

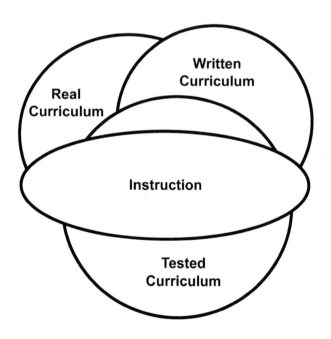

As textbooks are being selected, learning objectives and goals (both local and state) are examined. During this examination process, teachers:

♦ Modify goals and objectives based on recency (when necessary);

♦ Select textbooks and other resources necessary to meet content goals; and,

♦ Refine district curriculum guides.

When these tasks (and perhaps others) have been completed, the written curriculum is in place. The taught curriculum develops as a result of what teachers do in their classrooms, making subtle changes to adapt the written curriculum to the needs of students and the context of the classroom.

From a practice perspective, there is a critical area that links the real, written, and tested curricula—instructional strategies used to deliver the curricula. Varying instructional strategies utilized to bring life to the curriculum are especially critical in the block. With extended periods of time, teachers in the block need to use, perhaps, three or four different strategies per block to sustain students' engagement in learning.

The impact and effectiveness of the real and written curricula, coupled with the impact of instruction, are measured within the sphere of the tested curriculum. The tested curriculum occurs at multiple stages:

♦ Daily assessment associated with teaching (live interaction);

♦ Teacher-driven formal assessments such as daily quizzes, chapter/unit tests, midterm/final examinations, presentation of portfolios, a mock trial, a reenactment of a major historical event; and,

♦ State mandated tests.

Understanding the existence of the various curricula is essential when restructuring for the block.

## CURRICULUM MAPPING

Curriculum mapping is a method of depicting the real curriculum. Curriculum maps can be designed to represent a multiyear sequence of courses (e.g., English I, English II, English III, and English IV), a specific course over a year/semester, or a single class period. All three can be particularly valuable when preparing for the transition to block scheduling. It is important to remember that curriculum mapping is a tool for *program* evaluation, not *teacher* evaluation. However, a supervisor or peer coach could help a teacher map his/her class period by noting such items as instructional strategies utilized and their duration. By working with another individual, the teacher would not become burdened with tracking information while teaching. The purpose of curriculum mapping is to determine what is being taught, how it is being taught, and the amount of class time expended to teach it.

The curriculum map in Figure 4.5 depicts a course for one week and provides data about precisely what teaching strategies are being utilized to teach concepts and over what period of time.

By analyzing the data collected through the mapping process, teachers can become more informed about preparing to teach in the block. When teachers map their teaching, the aggregation of data comprises a solid foundation for planning further staff development and pinpointing specific ways supervisors can be of assistance. Effective principals empower teachers by valuing their voice in making data-driven decisions concerning what staff development is needed. This process should include:

♦ Teachers discussing their findings with colleagues across subject levels;

♦ Teachers identifying commonalties; and then,

♦ Teachers designing staff development activities based on these findings.

**FIGURE 4.5. SAMPLE WEEKLY CURRICULUM MAP**

| | Topic Taught | Strategies Used | | Duration | Cumulative Time Totals |
|---|---|---|---|---|---|
| Monday Jan 11 | Causes of World War I | Lecture: | How it started | 15 min. | L = 15 |
| | | Pairs: | Arrange list of events in chronological order | 15 min. | C = 40 |
| | People and Places of World War I | Groups: | Worksheet/map, World War I | 25 min. | |
| Tuesday Jan 12 | Central Powers | Lecture: | Which country goes where? | 10 min. | L = 25 |
| | Triple Alliance | Groups: | Mock war planning conference | 35 min. | C = 75 |
| | Triple Entente | Discussion: | Politics and World War I | 10 min. | D = 10 |
| Wednesday Jan 13 | Battle of the Marne and the Battle of Verdun | Lecture: | Setting the scene | 10 min. | L = 35 |
| | | Simulation: | Battle Planning Conference | 30 min. | C = 75 |
| | | Discussion: | What would you have done differently? | 1 min. | D = 25 |
| | | | | | S = 30 |

**FIGURE 4.5. SAMPLE WEEKLY CURRICULUM MAP, CONTINUED**

| | Topic Taught | Strategies Used | | Duration | Cumulative Time Totals |
|---|---|---|---|---|---|
| Thursday Jan 14 | Russian Revolution and American Entry into World War I | *Lecture:* | Connecting the two events | 10 min. | L = 45 |
| | | *Groups:* | Worksheets on Russian Revolution | 15 min. | C = 90 |
| | | | | | D = 55 |
| | | *Discussion:* | Was America obliged to enter World War I? | 30 min. | S = 30 |
| Friday Jan 15 | The Treaty of Versailles | *Lecture:* | Setting the stage | 5 min. | L = 50 |
| | | *Simulation:* | Reenactment of the Versailles Peace Conference | 40 min. | C = 90 |
| | | | | | D = 65 |
| | | *Discussion:* | Wrap-up | 10 min. | S = 70 |

Legend: L = Lecture; C = Cooperative Learning; D = Discussion; S = Simulations

## PACING GUIDES

A major challenge faced by teachers new to the block is learning to restructure a course from a 180-day, 36-week format to one compatible with the new schedule. While nearly all instructional manuals include scope and sequence charts to assist the teacher in planning course content, each form of block schedule (i.e., accelerated, alternating, and Copernican) brings unique time considerations. The development of pacing guides can help reduce teacher anxiety by helping them restructure the content of courses for the new schedule (North Carolina State Department of Public Instruction, 1997). Pacing guides can assist teachers in organizing information such as topics to be included, correlation to state/district objectives, corresponding pages in the textbook, time needed for completion, and resources needed. Figure 4.6 provides a sample form for developing a pacing guide.

Pacing guides take time to complete. Principals can help by arranging release time for teachers, extending planning periods, or allowing teachers to use faculty meeting time. Teachers new to the block can be seduced by the allure of the *extra* time in each class period. Without being aware, much of the semester can evaporate without sufficient content being taught. A well-developed pacing guide can help teachers avoid this trap.

### INSTRUCTIONAL PACING

The implementation of multiple teaching strategies and transitions creates the need for teachers to be able to pace instruction within each block period. Although still flexible, teachers need to plan how long each learning activity should last and how the transitions from one activity to the next will occur. Figures 4.7 to 4.12 are sample instructional pacing guides, each depicting a single class period with approximate times for each activity.

Instructional supervision (administrative or peer driven) can be enhanced by utilizing content/instructional pacing techniques. With the teacher and supervisor (or peer coach) collecting data about content pacing and instructional strategies, more informed decisions can be made regarding pacing, content coverage, and student outcomes.

*(Text continues on page 111.)*

## FIGURE 4.6. SAMPLE PACING GUIDE

Department: Mathematics     Course: Algebra II

| Topic | Correlating State Objective(s) | Textbook Pages | Resources Needed | Number of Days Needed |
|---|---|---|---|---|
| Graphing quadratic equations | II a, b, e | pp. 48–62 | Graphing calculators | 2 days |
| Solving real-life application problems using quadratic equations | IV b, c; V a | pp. 63–74 | Graphing calculators, textbook | 1 day |
| Write/present problems that require quadratic equations to solve | Ia; II b, c | | Markers, flip charts, videotapes | 2 days |

## FIGURE 4.7. SAMPLE INSTRUCTIONAL PACING GUIDE: GEOMETRY

**Teacher:** Jones

**Course:** Geometry

**Date:** September, 18, 1999

**Objective(s):** Classification of Triangles and their Properties

**State/District Objective Correlation:** II a, b, d

| *Classroom Events* | *Anticipated Time Needed* |
|---|---|
| • **Explanation**<br><br>Introductory Activity: Discussion of Practical Applications of triangles in areas such as surveying, construction, and sports. | 10 minutes |
| • **Application**<br>    **Learning Activities/Methodologies**<br><br>1. Cooperative Learning: Students will construct triangles according to instructions on chalkboard, using pencil, straightedge, and compass. | 25 minutes |
| 2. Cooperative Learning/Inquiry: Students will use protractor and ruler to measure all angles and sides within each triangle. | 20 minutes |
| • **Transition Strategies**<br><br>1. Teacher-led discussion to determine what characteristics should be used to classify triangles and to introduce needed terminology. | 5 minutes |
| 2. Teacher will solicit group input concerning patterns discovered during Learning Activity #2 | 5 minutes |

| | |
|---|---|
| • **Monitoring Strategies**<br><br>Teacher will monitor student learning through questioning and monitoring by walking around. | N/A |
| • **Assessment Strategies**<br><br>1. Student constructions will be placed in portfolios. | 5 minutes |
| • **Closure**<br><br>Discuss how right angles may be used to construct a baseball field and how those right angles are related to tomorrow's topic: the square. | 10 minutes |
| *Total Time Used* | 80 minutes |

### FIGURE 4.8. SAMPLE INSTRUCTIONAL PACING GUIDE: ENGLISH I

**Teacher:** Andrews

**Course:** English I

**Date:** September, 18, 1999

**Objective(s):** Distinguishing fact from fiction and identifying propaganda in *The Diary of Anne Frank*

**State/District Objective Correlation:** I a, IIb, d, IIIc

| *Classroom Events* | *Anticipated Time Needed* |
|---|---|
| • **Explanation**<br>Introductory Activity: Discussion of what differentiates fact from fiction and what constitutes propaganda. | 10 minutes |
| • **Application**<br>   **Learning Activities/Methodologies**<br><br>1. Socratic Seminar: students will participate in a Socratic Seminar discussing examples of opinion from assigned pages of *The Diary of Anne Frank*. | 40 minutes |
| 2. Cooperative Learning: Students will then rewrite selected passages replacing the opinion with relevant facts. | 15 minutes |
| • **Transition Strategies**<br><br>1. Teacher-led discussion to determine how fact and opinion relate to propaganda. Teacher will solicit group input based on Learning Activity #1. | 3 minutes |

| | |
|---|---|
| • **Monitoring Strategies**<br><br>Teacher will monitor student learning through questioning during the seminar and monitoring by walking around during the cooperative learning writing activity. | N/A |
| • **Assessment Strategies**<br><br>1.  Student constructions will be corrected and placed in portfolios. | 5 minutes |
| • **Closure**<br><br>Discuss how propaganda and opinion are used in society today (e.g., advertising, politics). | 7 minutes |
| ***Total Time Used*** | 80 minutes |

### FIGURE 4.9. SAMPLE INSTRUCTIONAL PACING GUIDE: WORLD GEOGRAPHY

**Teacher:** Crenshaw

**Course:** World Geography

**Date:** September, 18, 1999

**Objective(s):** Identify the major geographic regions of South America and how that geography effects the lives of South Americans.

**State/District Objective Correlation:** II a, b, d

| Classroom Events | Anticipated Time Needed |
|---|---|
| • **Explanation**<br><br>Introductory Activity: Using a physical map of South America lead students in a discussion which will identify major geographic landmarks (e.g., the Andes, the Amazon River). | 10 minutes |
| • **Application**<br><br>**Learning Activities/Methodologies**<br><br>1. Cooperative Learning: Using outline maps of South America, student will locate a list of geographic landmarks, and then write an essay describing how these landmarks can be barriers to the natives' progress. Each group discusses an assigned sector of society (e.g., socialization, industry) | 35 minutes |
| 2. Inquiry: Students investigate possible solutions to a problem of industry posed by geography. | 10 minutes |

| | |
|---|---|
| • **Transition Strategies** | |
| 1. As student prepare for Learning Activity #2, teacher will review nations and capitals of South America by using a question and answer sequence. | 5 minutes |
| 2. Teacher will solicit group input concerning patterns discovered during Learning Activity #2. | 5 minutes |
| • **Monitoring Strategies** | |
| Teacher will monitor student learning through questioning. | N/A |
| • **Assessment Strategies** | |
| 1. Student essays will be corrected and placed in portfolios. | 5 minutes |
| • **Closure** | |
| Discuss ways in which the Andes effected how the people of Columbia cultivated their land. Then introduce tomorrow's topic: economic development of South America. | 10 minutes |
| *Total Time Used* | 80 minutes |

### FIGURE 4.10. SAMPLE INSTRUCTIONAL PACING GUIDE: FRENCH I

**Teacher:** Hitchcock

**Course:** French I

**Date:** September, 18, 1999

**Objective(s):** Telling Time

**State/District Objective Correlation:** IVb, d, Vc

| *Classroom Events* | *Anticipated Time Needed* |
|---|---|
| • **Explanation** <br><br> Introductory Activity: Students complete anagrams of colors (in French) by unscrambling words from overhead and writing definitions of each. Directions given for first activity. | 10 minutes |
| • **Application** <br> **Learning Activities/Methodologies** <br><br> 1. Lecture: teacher demonstrates telling time and has students imitate. | 15 minutes |
| 2. Cooperative Learning: Students practice (in pairs) dialogue that includes telling time material just covered. Students then perform their dialogues for a grade. | 20 minutes |
| 3. Cooperative Learning: Students write and then perform their own dialogues using vocabulary involving times and days of the week. | 15 minutes |
| • **Transition Strategies** <br> 1. Teacher-led Q&A sequence in French (Telling Time). | 5 minutes |

| | |
|---|---|
| • **Monitoring Strategies**<br><br>Teacher will monitor student learning by walking around and through listening to and speaking with students. | N/A |
| • **Assessment Strategies**<br><br>1. Student dialogue scripts will be corrected and placed in portfolios. | 5 minutes |
| • **Closure**<br><br>Use dialogue for setting an appointment to link telling time to tomorrow's objective: days of the week and months of the year. | 10 minutes |
| *Total Time Used* | 80 minutes |

### FIGURE 4.11. SAMPLE INSTRUCTIONAL PACING GUIDE: MUSIC

**Teacher:** Webber

**Course:** Music

**Date:** September, 18, 1999

**Objective(s):** Performance of Motets

**State/District Objective Correlation:** Ia, IIb, d, IIIc

| Classroom Events | Anticipated Time Needed |
|---|---|
| • **Explanation**<br>Introductory Activity: Vocalises (vocal exercises) | 5 minutes |
| • **Application**<br>**Learning Activities/Methodologies**<br><br>1. Group Discussion: What is a motet? Who are the important composers of motets? | 5 minutes |
| 2. Cooperative Learning: Sectional Rehearsals | 10 minutes |
| 3. Group Rehearsal | 45 minutes |
| • **Transition Strategies**<br><br>1. Announcements concerning upcoming concert | 5 minutes |
| • **Monitoring Strategies**<br>Teacher will monitor student learning through listening during the sectional rehearsals and group rehearsal. Teacher will also use some question and answer sequences. | N/A |

| | |
|---|---|
| • **Assessment Strategies** | |
| 1. Student progress will be assessed based on effort and cooperation. | N/A |
| • **Closure** | |
| Review characteristics of a motet. | 10 minutes |
| *Total Time Used* | 80 minutes |

## FIGURE 4.12. SAMPLE INSTRUCTIONAL PACING GUIDE: COMPUTER SCIENCE

**Teacher:** Watson

**Course:** Computer Science

**Date:** September, 18, 1999

**Objective(s):** Write a Program to Balance a Checkbook

**State/District Objective Correlation:** IIb, d, VIIc

| Classroom Events | Anticipated Time Needed |
|---|---|
| • **Explanation**<br>Class discussion: Why is it important to be able to balance your checkbook with a computer? | 10 minutes |
| • **Application**<br>**Learning Activities/Methodologies**<br>1. Lecture: Syntax necessary to write the program and common errors to avoid. | 10 minutes |
| 2. Independent Learning: Write the program using syntax discussed. Then run the program as a check for errors. | 25 minutes |
| 3. Cooperative Learning: Once program has run successfully, in small groups, students will write an addition to the program that will compute interest on this account. | 10 minutes |
| • **Transition Strategies**<br>1. Teacher will transition between learning activities by questioning students to reinforce new syntax learned. | 5 minutes |

| | |
|---|---|
| • **Monitoring Strategies**<br><br>Teacher will monitor student learning through questioning and spot inspection of computer programs. | N/A |
| • **Assessment Strategies**<br><br>1. Student programs will be tested by being run on the computer. Printouts will be placed in portfolios. | 10 minutes |
| • **Closure**<br><br>Discuss how the program written today could be enlarged to track accounts for a bank. What modifications might be needed? | 10 minutes |
| *Total Time Used* | 80 minutes |

Data collected by auditing provides a firm foundation for teachers to make informed decisions concerning their professional practice. For example, a physics teacher, concerned about her/ his students' scores on state mandated achievement tests, could use auditing techniques to determine which objectives are being covered in her/his class, and what instructional strategies are being used to deliver these objectives. Next, the teacher could examine the available achievement test data to discern any objectives that consistently gave students difficulty.

By comparing data from the audit with data from the achievement test, the teacher could identify information useful for formulating an action plan to improve her/his teaching. In this instance, audits have led to action research. Such information can also help identify staff development needs and focus areas for future classroom observations. Hence, the intertwined nature of supervision and staff development can be of benefit to this teacher's self-examination of practice. Figure 4.13 offers an illustration of how this data might look.

### FIGURE 4.13. INSTRUCTIONAL AUDIT FORM

| Problem Objectives | Curriculum Map | Pacing Guide | Instructional Strategies Used |
|---|---|---|---|
| 1. Newton's Laws of Motion | Unit 1, Objectives d-f | 3 days | Cooperative Learning |
| 2. Calculating velocity of projectiles | Unit 3, Objective a-c | 2 days | Cooperative Learning |

After reviewing the above data, the teacher and/or supervisor could identify, as a goal, refining skills in facilitating cooperative learning and, perhaps, as a focus for future classroom observations.

## INITIATIVES THAT FORWARD PREPARATION FOR TEACHING IN THE BLOCK

There is a compelling temptation for school leaders to believe that once block scheduling has been researched and a scheduling format selected the restructuring of time is essentially complete. The transition from traditional to block scheduling takes place on two levels: the macro level and the micro level. On the macro level, stakeholders' research and study block scheduling with the immediate goal of transforming the school's master teaching schedule. The micro level consists of the staff development and supervisory initiatives needed to transform teaching within the new time block adopted. Wyatt (1996) believes that:

> Something far more significant has to occur than just adding more time to secondary school classes to live up to the expectations...about the results of teaching in the block. That significant something hinges on the staff development of teachers. (p. 16)

In addition to auditing techniques such as curriculum mapping and pacing instruction, staff development initiatives that can forward preparation for a block schedule include site visitations and specified in-services to facilitate learning new teaching and student assessment strategies.

### SITE VISITATIONS

While generalizing about adult learning can be somewhat hazardous, Brookfield (1986) asserts that adults:

- Use personal experience as a learning resource;
- Prefer their learning to center around real life tasks; and,
- Desire a *hands-on* approach to learning.

These principles offer support for the value of including site visits to schools currently on a block schedule. There are two major benefits of site visits: the opportunity to *observe* teaching in the context of a block schedule and time for professional *dialogue*.

Professional literature concerning block scheduling is replete with suggested strategies for implementing a block schedule and teaching strategies useful during extended class periods. However, first-hand observation of an experienced *block* teacher provides a vantage point for learning that too often escapes the written word.

## BUILDING BLOCK:
## TIPS FOR CLASSROOM
## OBSERVATIONS DURING SITE VISITS

While observing an experienced *block* teacher, be sure to watch for teacher-student interactions during learning activities, the orchestration of transitions from one activity to another, and differentiated strategies for monitoring and assessing learning.

The significance of professional dialogue is supported by adults' need to learn in a social environment where knowledge can be self-constructed (Brooks & Brooks, 1993). When fused with the rich learning reservoir of personal experience, dialogue offers teachers the opportunity to share successes and concerns about their practice and provides a mechanism for curricular decision making (Arnold, 1995).

For site visits to be possible, principals need to provide release time for teachers. Because it is impractical to release every teacher, time for informal and formal discussion within departments or teams should also be provided so that teachers who have gone on site visits can share what they have learned. Through personal observation of an experienced block teacher, the newcomer has the opportunity to experience a live demonstration of teaching in the block and, time permitting, an opportunity to ask questions.

The principal is encouraged to provide release time for teams of teachers to make site visitations. Team composition should include a cross representation of leadership from among the staff.

---

### BUILDING BLOCK:
### MAKING THE BEST USE OF
### FACULTY MEETINGS

Use faculty meetings as a weekly staff development activity by forming cluster groups to facilitate dialogue about teaching. Make sure that faculty who have been on site visits are distributed throughout the groups. Faculty meetings are also excellent forums for planning future activities such as follow-up on large and small group work.

---

## NEW TEACHING STRATEGIES AND IN-SERVICE

Canady and Rettig (1995) describe block scheduling as a catalyst for teachers to explore innovative teaching strategies. Quickly emphasized, however, is the assertion that the initial process of preparing teachers to teach in the block takes time; at least five days of intensive in-service is recommended *before* the first day of teaching (p. 205).

For the purposes of this book, in-service and staff development are not used interchangeably. Zepeda (1999a) defines *in-service* as job-oriented activities that are designed to address immediate, specific needs. Staff development is people oriented. It is a comprehensive plan to enhance the growth of the entire faculty. Staff development plans are designed to address long-range goals. In-service can and should be a part of a site or district staff development plan.

Effective staff development and supervision reflect adult learning principles and utilize active rather than passive methods. *Sit and get* workshops by themselves will not ensure transfer of newly learned skills into practice. Infusing active learning strategies such as simulations and role-playing, coupled with constructive feedback, enhance the effectiveness of workshops. In-service alone cannot be expected to prepare teachers for the block. A clearly defined, long-term staff development program is essential to both initiating and maintaining a block schedule.

Initial and ongoing staff development needs to prepare teachers for block scheduling by providing skill development in:

♦ Planning lessons;

♦ Varying instructional strategies;

♦ Organizing the classroom; and,

♦ Using differentiated assessment techniques.

### LESSON PLANNING

When planning lessons for the block schedule, a natural tendency is to plan two lessons per block period. It is important to realize that the purpose of block scheduling is to provide longer blocks of time to study topics in more depth, not merely to allow a rearrangement of existing content. Wyatt (1996) describes this phenomenon as "less content but greater mastery" (p. 17).

Canady and Rettig (1995) recommend dividing class periods into three segments:

♦ Explanation gives directions and disseminates new information;

♦ Application extends new knowledge through diverse learning activities; and,

♦ Synthesis connects explanation to application, followed by closure (pp. 206–209).

These class segments are, of course, filled with many activities such as lecture, discussion, activities (small and large group), question and answer sequences, and multiple demonstrations of skill and content mastery.

A tool that can be helpful in assisting teachers organize instruction for block periods is a lesson-planning guide. A lesson-planning guide helps teachers better plan what instruction will drive the content to be taught. This type of planning tool focuses on instructional methods and activities, transitions, monitoring strategies, assessment procedures, and closure. Figure 4.14 illustrates a typical lesson plan form for a block schedule.

**FIGURE 4.14. SAMPLE LESSON PLAN FORM FOR
CLASS IN THE BLOCK SCHEDULE**

| |
|---|
| Teacher:<br>Course:<br>Date: |
| Objective(s)<br><br>State/District Objective Correlation: |
| Explanation<br>Introductory Activity: |
| Application<br>Learning Activities/Methods to be used (need at least two, preferably three):<br><br>Transition Strategies:<br><br>Monitoring Strategies:<br><br>Assessment Strategies: |
| Synthesis<br>Individual Practice:<br><br><br>Closure: |

Lesson planning will require teachers to think more about time—the amount of instructional time, the time allotted for student learning activities, and time for assessments such as simulations, group presentations, and individual demonstrations.

## VARYING INSTRUCTIONAL STRATEGIES

Teachers need the opportunity to learn new teaching skills. Using curriculum maps (see Figure 4.5, pp. 95-96), teachers will be able to identify those strategies with which they are comfortable, and those that they need to practice. Effective teaching strategies in the block include Socratic seminars, cooperative learning, simulations, development of learning centers, technology-based lessons, inquiry, and puzzles/games/manipulatives (Canady & Rettig, 1995; Gilkey & Hunt, 1998). Each learning activity should include a strategy to assess its effectiveness.

## TRANSITIONS

With the advent of new instructional strategies and longer class periods comes the need to learn how to transition from one class activity to another. Block lessons begin to disintegrate when one learning activity has ended and the next has yet to begin. Transitions can take the form of verbal cues, learning centers, short daily quizzes, or puzzles. Managing transitions between segments is key to keeping students on task and avoiding opportunity for students to disrupt the *hum of learning*.

## CLASSROOM ORGANIZATION

### PHYSICAL SPACE

Classroom organization refers to the arrangement of furniture and equipment, as well as the order of activities in a given class period. All facets of the class need to complement the lesson that is being taught. Cooperative learning, learning centers, and laboratory activities require specific arrangement of equipment. These activities need to be negotiated in order to know what activities will be done and by whom.

### SEATWORK AND HOMEWORK

Teachers new to the block also need to decide how they will manage homework. How much homework should be assigned and how often? This will depend on the type of course and the form of scheduling. Homework assignments designed for an accelerated block might be different from those developed for an alternating block. A perennial issue is whether teachers should give class time for completing homework assignments. While independent practice is an important tool for learning, teachers should be cautious about using too much class time for homework completion. Although the teacher may use homework as an additional opportunity to monitor student learning, teachers need to be careful not to turn algebra or biology class into a study hall.

## CLASSROOM BREAKS

Also to be decided is the issue of breaks. Because of the communal nature of school facilities, this question needs to be addressed by the faculty as a group. If classes are to be allowed to take breaks outside of the classroom, this clearly adds the task of monitoring the hallways. The possibility of increased disciplinary contacts created by the additional student presence in the halls must be weighed against any perceived benefit of having breaks.

# DIFFERENTIATED TECHNIQUES FOR ASSESSING STUDENT LEARNING

Assessment of student mastery needs to be a part of staff development for the block. The use of diverse teaching methods necessitates the use of equally diverse assessment techniques. While pencil and paper tests can still be useful for evaluating student mastery of some skills, using alternative assessment strategies permits students with diverse learning styles to demonstrate what they have learned. Assessment strategies include portfolios, demonstrations, and research projects.

## PORTFOLIOS

A portfolio is a collection of artifacts such as essays, drawings, letters, and posters that demonstrate that a student has mastered an objective. Portfolios are particularly useful for assessing progress over an extended period of time such as an entire grading period. As alternative assessment, portfolios offer several advantages over pencil and paper tests. Brown (1997) identifies these advantages:

♦ Provides teachers with important information for diagnosing student weaknesses;

♦ Helps students see gaps in their own learning; and,

♦ Involves students in the assessment of their learning. (p. 3)

Murphy (1997) believes that an important quality of portfolio assessment is that it is both formative and summative. Given the ongoing (formative) nature of portfolio construction, the development of the portfolio allows teachers and students to diagnose and remediate weaknesses as learning is occurring instead of waiting until the very end of a unit, quarter, or semester. To this end, adjustments to instructional and learning activities can be made. A long-term view of the portfolio is to extend the development of portfolios over more than one year. For example, students in English I would transport their portfolios to English II and beyond.

The utilization of the portfolio over an extended period of time can provide a powerful view of learning for both the student and the teacher. Instruction can be enhanced with informed modifications made through the results gleaned from examining the content of student portfolios.

Portfolio examination can provide opportunities for teachers to conduct action research about their teaching and its impact on student gains in learning after the efforts of instruction. Student work should reflect content, instruction, analysis, and interpretation. After reviewing student work, teachers can analyze cumulative gains in students' progress against instructional approaches.

To build on the English I portfolio example, the portfolio, if used by several teachers at the same grade level, can help assess the overall curriculum and its impact. Through this type of action research—the auditing techniques suggested in this chapter—teachers can assess course content, instructional strategies, learning activities, pacing, and assessment techniques. By examining these areas, teachers will be able to learn from one another and, through dialogue, become better teachers. Action research is more thoroughly discussed in Chapter 6.

### DEMONSTRATIONS

Demonstrations have traditionally been the domain of electives such as music, drama, and industrial arts. However, demonstrations can be effective assessment tools of simulations and cooperative learning across all core courses. For example, following a unit on finding area, a geometry teacher could have students demonstrate mastery of content by developing and presenting an original practical application problem such as determining the area of an irregularly shaped lake. The presentation should include necessary calculations and a narrative explaining what type of practitioner (e.g., surveyor, architect) would need to know how to solve this problem and why.

### RESEARCH PROJECTS

Research projects can provide useful data for student assessment in a variety of settings. In place of a pencil and paper test, a physical science teacher might have students collect and test soil samples from the surrounding area to demonstrate understanding of local erosion problems. Included in this project could be a formal paper reporting the results, a class presentation/demonstration, and peer as well as teacher assessment of a presentation or demonstration.

## TEACHING STRATEGIES THAT ENHANCE LEARNING IN BLOCK PERIODS

Probably few people have been spared the experience of trying to be attentive to a speaker who does not seem to know when to stop. The same principle applies to the classroom. Attempting to lecture for 80 minutes or more is difficult for the teacher as well as the students. Varied instructional strategies become an indispensable part of the teacher's *toolkit* when preparing to teach in the block.

It is not possible within the limitations of this chapter to provide complete information on any one teaching strategy. This section is provided as an introduction to alternative instructional strategies for the block classroom. You are encouraged to consult the sources provided at the end of this chapter for further information.

## SOCRATIC SEMINARS

A Socratic seminar is a structured class dialogue in which the teacher and student alike serve as both facilitator and participant. A text for discussion is selected by the teacher and read by both the teacher and the students. The seminar begins with an opening question designed by the teacher to introduce main themes of the text or possible topics for discussion (Canady & Rettig, 1995). The opening question should be open-ended to encourage discussion.

Following the opening question, students discuss the themes of the text, and they are required to support their positions with passages from within the text. To sustain the momentum of the discussion, the teacher prepares two to five *core questions* that ask students to take a position on an issue and to support that position with passages from the text. Teacher-generated questions for the Socratic seminar need to be value free. Students should be encouraged to make and defend their own judgments.

The last phase of the Socratic seminar consists of a final question that encourages the students to apply what they have learned to the real world. For example, a history class studying World War II might use Chapter 12, "The Road to Munich," from William L. Shirer's *The Rise and Fall of the Third Reich* to investigate how Hitler's dishonesty with various political leaders affected the course of world events. Students could then transfer their newly constructed knowledge of the consequences of deception to student leaders and their roles in school organizations.

Socratic seminars benefit student learning by:

♦ Providing opportunity for students to be leaders in their own learning;

♦ Requiring students to use higher order thinking skills; and,

♦ Allowing students to construct knowledge free of value judgments.

To facilitate discussion and to establish that all participants (including the teacher) *hold the same rank*, it is recommended that chairs be moved to form a circle. This arrangement also makes eye contact easier (Ball and Brewer, 1996).

## COOPERATIVE LEARNING

Johnson and Johnson (1994) define cooperative learning as:

> Students working together...to achieve shared learning goals and to complete specific tasks and assignments. These assignments include decision making or problem solving, completing a curriculum unit, writing a report, conducting a survey or experiment, reading a chapter or reference book, learning vocabulary, or answering questions at the end of the chapter. (p. 52)

Kagan (1992) identifies five essential steps for implementing cooperative learning:

♦ Class building—students need to become acquainted with one another prior to being divided into groups;

♦ Team formation—students are divided into teams of usually three or four members either by teacher, student, or random selection;

♦ Team building and identity—teams become acquainted with one another through *ice breaker* activities and then develop team identity with a name or logo;

♦ Cooperative learning structures—learning activities completed by the team with every member having his or her specific responsibility (e.g., recorder or researcher) are essential to ensure involvement by all members; and,

♦ Group processing and evaluation—students along with the teacher evaluate each member's contribution. Peer evaluation and self-evaluation are encouraged.

Cooperative learning yields many benefits to student learning—positive interdependence; face-to-face interactions; individual accountability; and development of social and group processing skills (Johnson & Johnson, 1994). According to Sharan and Sharan (1976), cooperative learning is most successful when the role of the teacher changes:

> An active planning-and learning role for the student necessitates a complementary change in the role of the teacher. From being a dispenser and transmitter of knowledge, he becomes a guide and advisor to students. He helps them investigate issues and clarify and solve problems; but he is not the main source of information.... (pp. 4–5)

### THE TEACHER'S ROLE IN COOPERATIVE LEARNING

In cooperative learning, the teacher assumes responsibility for:

♦ Specifying objectives for the lesson: both an academic and a social skills objective should be specified;

♦ Making pre-instructional decisions: these decisions include size of groups, how students will be assigned to groups, what materials will be needed, and how the room will be arranged;

♦ Explaining the task and positive interdependence: the assignment is clearly defined including explanation of required concepts to be used, criteria for success, and individual accountability. Positive interdependence is emphasized;

♦ Monitoring students' learning and intervening within the groups: through monitoring their activities, the teacher will be able to determine individual student involvement. When necessary, the teacher intervenes to facilitate completion of task and interaction patterns of the group; and,

♦ Evaluating students' learning and helping students process how well their group functioned: both student learning and group interaction are evaluated by the teacher, followed by student evaluation. (Johnson & Johnson, 1994)

### THE STUDENT'S ROLE IN COOPERATIVE LEARNING

Students also have responsibilities to ensure successful implementation of cooperative learning. Johnson and Johnson (1990) conclude that students must:

♦ Get to know and trust one another;

♦ Communicate accurately and unambiguously;

♦ Accept and support one another; and,

♦ Resolve conflicts constructively. (p. 30)

Johnson and Johnson (1990) identify the following as necessary social skills for cooperative learning: staying with the group, using quiet voices, giving direction to the group's work, encouraging participation, explaining answers, and criticizing ideas without criticizing people. Through monitoring group work, the teacher can help students learn the necessary social skills needed to focus learning in the cooperative learning model.

### TYPES OF COOPERATIVE LEARNING

Johnson, Johnson, and Smith (1991) identify four major types of cooperative learning. *Formal cooperative learning* consists of groups that work on assignments over the span of several class periods. *Informal cooperative learning groups* work on tasks for only a class period or less. The membership of these groups is often reformulated. *Cooperative base groups* are heterogeneous groups that can last over a period of several school years and meet formally a day or two per week. The purpose of the cooperative base group is to provide peer support for student learning.

*Cooperative learning structures* are structures developed to manage classroom routines. Think/pair/share, often shortened to TPS, is one popular cooperative learning structure. The teacher asks students, who are working in pairs, questions. Each student is required to wait (think) 3 to 5 seconds before consulting his/her partner (pair), and then each pair communicates its answer to the rest of the class (share). This strategy is helpful in engaging more students in the learning process (Strebe, 1996).

## ASSESSING COOPERATIVE LEARNING

When assessing student learning while utilizing cooperative learning, each student should receive his/her own grade. Teacher workload is an argument in favor of group grading. However, Kagan (1995) makes a persuasive argument in supporting the necessity of individual grading. Group grades:

♦ Hold students accountable for circumstances beyond their control, namely the performance of classmates;

♦ Violate the principle of individual accountability;

♦ Create resistance in parents, teachers, and students to cooperative learning; and,

♦ May be challenged in court. (pp. 70–71)

## *SIMULATIONS*

Simulations are recreations of real world situations in which students, through role-play, are given the opportunity to apply content to a given problem. All core content areas (English, history, mathematics, and science) are replete with possibilities for simulations. For example, a history class might stage a mock trial, a science class could *race against the clock* in responding to an epidemic, or a mathematics class could use simple probability theory and statistics in a simulation of a research study.
Successful simulations require:

♦ A stated objective—students need to know what they are expected to learn from the exercise;

♦ Clearly defined roles for each student—a statement of what each student is expected to do and within what limitations (if any);

♦ Concisely written rules—what is and is not permitted within the confines of the simulation;

♦ Discussion questions—to provide closure for the lesson; and,

♦ A specific assessment rubric—to indicate how student performance will be assessed.

Simulations can be enhanced with field trips, guest speakers, and technology. Referring back to the mock trial example, a social studies class might visit a local court to gain firsthand knowledge of how a trial proceeds. A biology class that is studying microorganisms could invite a local physician, paramedic, or public health official to discuss disease control. English classes can enhance simulations by comparing a play to its motion picture counterpart prior to creating their own screenplay based on a selection they have read.

Simulations also provide an excellent platform for designing interdisciplinary lessons. A mock trial can involve mathematics and science classes as *expert witnesses*, journalism classes are *press pools*, and debate students can be excellent coaches for attorneys. Teachers should be warned that preparing for simulations can be a time-consuming process; however, the benefits to student learning are well worth the effort.

### LEARNING CENTERS

The use of learning centers has long been a staple at the elementary level. In contrast, relatively few high school teachers have included this approach as part of their instructional repertoire. Examples of activities for high school learning centers include:

♦ Devices for measuring and calculating in a geometry class;

♦ Listening centers in a foreign language class;

♦ Materials and directions for the completion of a project for a home economics, art, or industrial arts class;

♦ Equipment for short experiments in a biology class; and,

♦ Packets containing short simulations of diplomatic problems in a history class. (Canady & Rettig, 1995, p. 234)

Learning centers can be used as a *transition* strategy. Students might visit two or three learning centers on the way from one major learning activity to another. Learning centers are also effective as enrichment for gifted/talented students (Winebrenner, 1992) and provide additional practice for students who might need extra assistance.

### TECHNOLOGY-BASED LESSONS

Technology offers a plethora of exciting instructional strategies for teachers and students. Through the magic of videotape, students can watch and interact with the major events of World War II instead of filling in worksheets about them. Graphics calculators in an algebra class can help bring to life the connection of equations and graphs to real life applications. With Internet access, a German class might take a virtual field trip to Berlin, a business mathematics class could track investments, and a history class might construct their family histories.

Tips for using technology in the classroom include:

♦ Advanced planning—ensure that needed equipment is available and that necessary background learning has been completed;

♦ State the learning objective—communicate what the student is expected to learn from the activity;

♦ Clear instructions—ensure that students know exactly what to do and in what sequence;

♦ Learning curve considerations—make sure that students know how to operate necessary equipment and software;

♦ Follow-up questions/activity—reinforce learning by providing students an activity that will encourage them to reflect on their learning; and,

♦ Assessment—decide how you will assess student performance and how students will be involved in the assessment (if at all).

## *INQUIRY*

The inquiry model of instruction has its roots in the science classroom. According to Suchman (1962), the purpose of inquiry is to "help children develop a set of skills and a broad schema for the investigation of causal relationships" (p. 3). The inquiry method consists of four main activities:

- ◆ Searching—the planned and controlled collection of data;
- ◆ Data processing—the organization of data in order to discern any patterns that may be present;
- ◆ Discovery—the process of seeing how data fits together; and,
- ◆ Verification—the *check* on the process of forming conclusions. (pp. 5–20)

Using the inquiry method, students are presented an open-ended assignment that becomes the foundation for student inquiry into learning objectives. For example, a mathematics teacher might use inquiry to introduce π (the symbol for the circumference of a circle divided by its diameter; see Figure 4.15).

---

**FIGURE 4.15. DIAMETER AND CIRCUMFERENCE OF A CIRCLE**

---

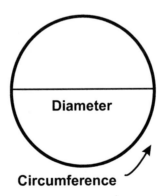

With students working in teams, have them measure the circumference and diameter of every circular object in the classroom. Next, the students could build a chart giving each set of measurements and their quotients. Students discover the secret ($\pi = 3.14$) because the last column of the chart should repeat an approximation of this number (see Figure 4.16). The closer the approximation in the last column, the more accurate the students' measurements are.

## FIGURE 4.16. SUMMARY CHART OF MEASUREMENTS

| Item | Diameter (D) | Circumference (C) | C ÷ D |
|------|--------------|-------------------|-------|
| Coffee Mug | 3" | 9.4" | 3.13 |
| Magic Marker | 0.75" | 2.4" | 3.20 |
| UHF TV Antenna | 7" | 22" | 3.143 |
| 12-ounce Soda Can | 2.3" | 7.2" | 3.13 |
| Wall Clock | 16" | 50.2 | 3.14 |

### THE TEACHER'S ROLE IN THE INQUIRY MODEL

Inquiry is a student-driven instructional model. Suchman (1962) established three main tasks for teachers when using the inquiry model:

- Establish and maintain procedures that students are to follow;
- Make new information available to students when needed; and,
- Guide the development of skills and strategies of students.

### THE PHASES OF THE INQUIRY MODEL

Joyce and Weil (1996) identify five phases of the inquiry model. In phase one, the students encounter the problem. After the teacher introduces the problem, students begin phase two, verification through data gathering, by asking *yes-no* questions to learn more about the problem. In phase three, students perform two tasks: exploration and direct testing. Exploration requires students to begin adding or deleting information from the data that they collected in phase two. As a result of direct testing, the students observe and record changes that occur as a result of the exploration task. Phase four requires students to form an explanation or theory based on data collected in phases two and three. In phase five, students analyze the process through which they formulated their explanation.

### TEACHING INQUIRY: WHAT TEACHERS NEED TO KNOW

Suchman (1962) described four essentials for successful teaching using the inquiry model:

- ◆ Concrete problems that are immediately intelligible to the learner—students need to be able to understand the problem with minimum explanation from the teacher;
- ◆ Freedom to perform data-gathering operations— learner control over how data is gathered and analyzed facilitates learner autonomy;
- ◆ A responsive environment—necessary data needs to be abundantly available to the learners; and,
- ◆ Elimination of extrinsic rewards—the sole motivation for inquiry should be to *find out why*. (p. 127)

### PUZZLES, GAMES, AND MANIPULATIVES

Puzzles and games can enhance any teacher's arsenal of instructional strategies. They can be icebreakers at the beginning of class, act as *downtime* learning between more intense learning activities, or as review at the end of a class period or unit. Puzzles are also easily embedded in other instructional strategies. For example, a history teacher could reinforce a lesson on the Civil War by developing a crossword puzzle in which the answers are Civil War generals or battles. Also, many popular board games are now available in foreign language editions. Formats of familiar television programs, such as *Jeopardy!*, are especially useful as review for assessments. Logic puzzles can be excellent tools for practicing problem-solving or critical thinking skills.

For visual learners, manipulatives can be helpful tools for students. Algebra tiles, for example, are used to depict quadratic equations using square and rectangular plastic pieces. When the pieces are assembled, students not only visualize the equation, but by examining its component blocks, students may also visualize its component factors.

Canady and Rettig (1995) recommend teachers plan at least three different learning activities for each block class. The preceding strategies can easily be adapted to enhance each teacher's repertoire. However, transfer of newly learned skills into practice tends to be a stumbling block for approximately 90% of teachers (Hirsh & Ponder, 1991). Traditional workshops alone do not ensure that this transfer takes place. A comprehensive staff development plan which is embedded in the daily work routine of teachers, is most effective (Wood & Killian, 1998).

## A COMPREHENSIVE STAFF DEVELOPMENT PLAN TO PREPARE TEACHERS FOR THE BLOCK

The goal of any staff development initiative is to bring about successful change by having its implementers (teachers) prepared. This is especially true with the implementation of a block schedule. To be fully prepared to teach in the block, teachers need time to learn new teaching strategies, realign curriculum, and practice what they have learned. For this reason, it is recommended that staff development for teachers preparing for the block begin at least one year in advance of implementation.

The following staff development plan is offered as a model only. Each school is encouraged to explore and make adjustments to fit its individual needs. Figure 4.17 offers an overview of a comprehensive staff development program for the year prior to implementation of a block schedule and for the year of implementation.

## FIGURE 4.17. A COMPREHENSIVE STAFF DEVELOPMENT PROGRAM FOR IMPLEMENTING A BLOCK SCHEDULE

### *Year One*

| *Time Frame* | *Event* | *Who Is Responsible* |
|---|---|---|
| August | Two-year plan formulated | Site staff development committee (SSDC) |
| | Study groups are formed to study relevant issues to teaching in the block and to develop check sheet for site visits. | Entire Faculty |
| August –October | Study groups report results during faculty meetings. | Teacher representatives from study groups |
| November –December | Site visits are conducted | Teachers and Administrators |
| January –March | Conduct 2–3 day staff development retreat that includes:<br>• Roundtable discussions on implications of the block for teaching and supervision;<br>• Workshops on specific teaching strategies (e.g., Socratic seminars, cooperative learning, inquiry, simulations), lesson planning, transition strategies, and classroom management; | SSDC; and experienced "block" teachers |

| *Time Frame* | *Event* | *Who Is Responsible* |
|---|---|---|
| | • Study group meetings; and, | |
| | • Time for identifying questions of practice and initiating action research. | |
| April–May | Conduct "trial run" block days in current schedule. | Faculty and Students |
| May | Staff Development Planning Conference | SSDC |
| | • Review of current years' Staff Development plan. | |
| | • Plan next years' Staff Development plan. | |

## Year Two

| | | |
|---|---|---|
| August | Conduct 2–3 day staff development retreat that includes: | SSDC |
| | • Roundtable discussions on implications of the block for teaching and supervision; | |
| | • Workshops (topics selected based on needs assessment conducted by SSDC) | |
| | • Study group meetings; and, | |
| | • Time for reviewing results of existing action research and identifying new action research. | |

| *Time Frame* | *Event* | *Who Is Responsible* |
| --- | --- | --- |
| August –May | Study groups and action research continues in departments and interdepartmentally. Faculty meetings should be used for study group and action research reports. | Faculty |
| January –March | One-day retreat for study group meetings, action research meetings, and informal dialogue by department or teams. | |
| May | Staff Development Planning Conference<br><br>• Review of current years' Staff Development plan.<br><br>• Plan next years' Staff Development plan. | SSDC |

School leaders should use Figure 4.17 as a "point of departure." The individual context of the school will determine exactly what its staff development plan needs to include. However, the following provides some guidance for designing a staff development plan:

♦ Study groups can be used to locate and collect relevant professional literature for study by the whole faculty, provide a forum for formal and informal dialogue, and to identify questions for initiating action research;

♦ Some events within the faculty retreats may be held at an alternative site. However, some of the subject-specific workshops should be held on campus so that teachers may "get the feel" of teaching in the block in their own classrooms;

♦ Roundtable discussions should address topics of general interest while workshops should be subject-specific (Canady & Rettig, 1995, p. 239);

♦ "Trial run" days (usually two) are formatted according to the specific schedule chosen by the school during which teachers and students receive "hands on" experience with block scheduling; and,

♦ The ways that instructional supervision and staff development will change as a result of the block schedule should be addressed during each of the faculty retreats.

Staff development and supervision are the underpinnings of successful change in schools. School leaders are in a unique position of redefining professional development activities in the block. As such, the type of administrative support and autonomy provided to teachers will determine, to a large extent, the type of learning community that will develop as a result of the combined interest and participation of all stakeholders.

## IMPLICATIONS

Teachers preparing to teach in a block schedule face many changes. Unless curriculum and instruction are retooled, a new schedule becomes nothing more than a new bell schedule. For gains in student learning to be realized, teachers need multiple learning opportunities, including follow-up, in order to refine new skills. To provide necessary learning for teachers, principals need to:

♦ Give teachers the latitude to analyze and to make decisions concerning their professional practices;

♦ Provide resources (e.g., release time, outside facilitators, access to professional literature) for continuous learning through appropriate staff development and supervision; and,

♦ Expand the role of teachers, department chairs, and curriculum coordinators in providing staff development and supervisory opportunities.

## SUMMARY

The implementation of a block schedule can act as the gateway to new avenues of professional development for teachers. However, developing new skills takes time and commitment. Effective principals facilitate faculty commitment by elevating the role of teachers to active participants in the decision-making process. Following a careful analysis of their professional practice through auditing strategies, teachers can become more informed about their own instructional practices.

Diverse staff development and supervisory activities such as role-playing, simulations, rehearsal, and coaching help principals to move their schools from isolated in-service meetings to a unified comprehensive staff development and supervision program that provides a more fertile learning environment. Only ongoing staff development and supervision, embedded in the daily work of teachers, can give them the opportunity to practice new skills necessary for implementing innovative instructional strategies.

For any change to be enduring, staff development to support that change must also be enduring. Zepeda (1999a) writes that:

> ...In-service is...job oriented; staff development is more person and process oriented. In-service has immediacy....Conversely, staff development provides thoughtful and guided enhancement of human talents and focuses on the attainment of long-range goals;...staff development promotes the continuous improvement of the total professional staff of the school system. (p. 4)

If instruction in the block is to improve, staff development and supervision to support teachers' learning must be ongoing and be embedded in the relevancy of their daily working lives. Moreover, staff development and supervision need to be linked in new ways. With a sustained staff development effort, the school can become a "community of learners" (Blase & Blase, 1998) whose focus is on student learning and organizational development (Zepeda, 1999a).

## SUGGESTED READINGS

Blase, J. R., & Blase, J. (1998) *Handbook of instructional leadership: How really good principals promote teaching and learning.* Thousand Oaks, CA: Corwin Press.

Canady, R. L., & Rettig, M. D. (Eds.). (1996). *Teaching in the block: Strategies for engaging active learners.* Larchmont, NY: Eye on Education.

Gainey, D. D., & Brucato, J. M. (1999). *Questions & answers about block scheduling: An implementation guide.* Larchmont, NY: Eye on Education.

Lybbert, B. (1998). *Transforming learning with block scheduling: A guide for principals.* Thousand Oaks, CA: Corwin Press.

Sparks, D., & Loucks-Horsley, S. (1989). Five models of staff development. *Journal of Staff Development, 10*(4), 40–57.

Wyatt, L. D. (1996). More time, more training: What staff development do teachers need for effective instruction in block scheduling? *The School Administrator, 58*(8), 16–18.

Zepeda, S. J. (1999a). *Staff development: Practices that promote leadership in learning communities.* Larchmont, NY: Eye on Education.

# 5

# SUPERVISION IN THE BLOCK: BLOCK: WHAT'S DIFFERENT

## CHAPTER OBJECTIVES

- ◆ Supervision in the block: What's different?
- ◆ Informal supervision and the block: New avenues for teacher growth.
- ◆ Track worthwhile trends in supervision and staff development in the block.

Supervision with the intent of promoting growth is critical in the block schedule (or, for that matter, in any schedule). The changes teachers will need to make in their instructional routines and behaviors, classroom management, and assessment practices will certainly be daunting tasks to go at alone. Here is where the efforts of the principal need to emerge. With leadership that is grounded in a commitment to improvement and a responsive style that attends to the developmental needs of teachers, the principal can make a difference in the instructional lives of their teachers.

This difference cannot be realized by supervision alone. A new position for supervision has to be created within the very structure of the school. This position needs to be more encompassing and tied to other processes that historically have not been united in any coherent fashion. Instructional supervision that is not tied to staff development processes (e.g., study groups, learning clusters, and teacher-led action research teams) will continue to remain a discrete activity that yields diminishing results in meeting teachers' learning needs.

Supervision needs to be conducted more collaboratively between teachers and principals, with each vested in growth and gains for both teachers and students. There are myriad *supervisory* formats (e.g., peer coaching) whose success are firmly grounded in teachers leading their own learning.

## SUPERVISION IN THE BLOCK: WHAT'S DIFFERENT?

### RETHINKING SUPERVISION

With the restructuring of time for students, teachers need shifts in the ways in which they learn about their own practices. Subsequently, principals need to begin rethinking instructional supervision (supervision that occurs in classrooms), classroom observation techniques, and the personnel who are involved. Processes that extend classroom observations are needed, along with learning activities that are embedded within teachers' workdays.

## EXTENDED TIME TO WORK WITH TEACHERS

Adult learning in the block schedule can only become meaningful if supervisory processes change to match the modifications in the master schedule. With longer class periods, classroom observations need to be extended. Many school districts have contract language and policies concerning classroom observations. It is not uncommon to find policies that state that a formal observation lasts the entire class session or for a prescribed amount of time (e.g., 50 minutes). If the contract language states that a classroom observation is to last the entire period, then the classroom observation in the block will last at least 90 minutes, depending on the type of schedule in place.

### BUILDING BLOCK
### EXAMINING SUPERVISION POLICY

If school district policy indicates that a classroom observation lasts for a prescribed number of minutes, then policy needs to be reexamined in light of the extended class period used in the block.

With an extended observation, the supervisor will need to be more familiar with the anticipated events to be observed in the classroom. It is only natural then for the pre-observation conference to last longer so that the supervisor and teacher have time to discuss learning objectives, instructional methods, learner characteristics, and, more importantly, the focus of the observation. Without a clear focus, the supervisor is apt to collect irrelevant data.

The post-observation conference is a critical process of supervision. It is during the post-observation conference that the teacher talks and reflects about learning from his/her own practices. The post-observation conference also requires more time to review data from an extended classroom observation.

## CLINICAL SUPERVISION

The instructional supervision model that most schools utilize is the clinical model that includes the pre-observation conference, the classroom observation, and the post-observation conference. This model, if properly applied, can:

♦ Foster dialogue;

♦ Affirm teachers' strengths;

♦ Assist teachers in identifying areas of instruction to bolster,

♦ Target areas for staff development; and,

♦ Encourage reflection.

## SUPERVISION IS NOT EVALUATION

Supervision is concerned with formative or ongoing growth. Too often, principals merely implement a supervisory model (clinical or otherwise) in order to meet district guidelines or state mandates that they evaluate teachers. When this occurs, supervision and evaluation often become confused as being one and the same. *Summative* evaluation signals whether or not the teacher will be retained or if a plan of improvement is necessary. At the end of the year, teachers are typically assigned a rating (e.g., *Excellent, Good, Satisfactory,* or *Unsatisfactory*). With a summative view, little professional growth can be expected. However, with a *formative* view, various supervisory models can be utilized to promote an ongoing exploration about teaching and learning.

McGreal (1983) believes that little growth occurs once a teacher is rated. That is, it is not the rating that promotes growth, but rather, what occurs before the final (summative) evaluation. The remainder of this chapter examines how classroom supervision and supervisory processes in the block can change to make learning more meaningful.

## SUPERVISION IN THE BLOCK

In a traditional high school schedule, the typical class period lasts between 48 and 54 minutes. In a block schedule, the typical class period lasts 90 or more minutes. For the principal, this time increase can appear overwhelming especially when considering the number of teachers to be supervised and the need, regardless of the model of supervision used in the school, to include time for the pre-observation conference, the observation, and the post-observation conference.

## THE PRE-OBSERVATION CONFERENCE

The pre-observation conference serves many functions. The classroom supervisory process, regardless of the type (e.g., clinical, coaching, peer) starts with a pre-observation conference. The pre-observation conference helps set the stage for the classroom observation. The pre-observation conference:

◆ Provides the teacher the opportunity to talk about teaching and student learning;

◆ Provides the teacher and supervisor time to pinpoint information about a specific lesson;

◆ Helps the supervisor understand the teacher's classroom environment;

◆ Assists the teacher in identifying one or two areas of practice to examine;

◆ Assists the supervisor in determining what data collection tools to use based on what areas of practice the teacher identifies; and,

◆ Defines the parameters of the observation: day, class period, and length of visitation.

The pre-observation conference should occur 24 hours before, or on the same day as, the observation, and should be conducted in the teacher's classroom. With a longer teaching period in the block, it is essential for the supervisor to follow the flow of instructional activities. There are several competing theories about whether the teacher, the supervisor, or the teacher and supervisor should direct the process of identifying the focus of the data collection during the observation. Unfortunately, there are no absolutes. Having as much information as possible prior to the observation, the supervisor will be in a better position to collect data that is reliable and pertinent to the teachers' needs. Figure 5.1 is a sample pre-observation form modified for the block.

**FIGURE 5.1. PRE-OBSERVATION CONFERENCE FORM
FOR THE BLOCK CLASSROOM**

## USA High School

Name_____ Grade Level/Subject _____

Pre-observation Date & Time _____ Classroom _____

Period/Block _____ Length of Visitation _____

Date, Period, & Classroom of Observation _____

Post-observation Date, Time, and Location _____

1. Curriculum:

    a. Unit (e.g., English I, The young adult novel and symbolism—*Rumblefish*):

    b. Lesson in unit (e.g., chapter 7—symbolism—Siamese Fighting Fish):

    c. Learning objectives for the unit (attach from curriculum guide if necessary):

    d. Learning objectives for the lesson:

    e. Place in the unit and lesson:

    f. Lesson artifacts:

2. Instruction:

    a. Instructional methods to be used (e.g., lecture, Q&A sequence):

    b. Learning activities planned (e.g., small and large groups, learning centers)

    c. Transitions between activities:

    d. Instructional materials to be used:

    e. Lesson artifacts:

3. Student Profile:

    a. Students with special needs:

    b. Academic range of students:

4. Assessment of Student Learning:

    a. What will students be doing?

    b. Monitoring strategies (e.g., how will you monitor student learning through instruction and learning activities?)

5. Teacher/Observer Focus: For what area (e.g., instruction, student response, classroom activities) would it be most beneficial for the teacher to have data for discussion and reflection in the post-observation conference?

---

Time can certainly be saved in the pre-observation conference by having the teacher fill out most of this information prior to the meeting; however, the teacher/observer focus should be filled out jointly with the observer. If the teacher elects to complete this form before the observation, the principal still needs to let the teacher *talk* him/her through the information. The principal's role is to let the teacher talk about teaching. Probing questions posed by the principal are encouraged so that he/she can see and hear the teacher mentally prepare what is written on the form. If the teacher brings this (or any other pre-observation) form blank, then the principal will need to record information as the teacher talks through the categories on this form.

Regardless of what form is used or who fills it out, it is essential to have the information presented in Figure 5.1 prior to the observation. Without this type of information, it is unlikely that data collected in the observation will be very meaningful for the teacher. Pre-observation conferences in the block will look and sound different because of the extended amount of time the principal will spend in the classroom observing the teacher. This extended time is well worth the effort. Getting supervision out of the office and conducting the pre-observation conference in the classroom can put the teacher more at ease and help the principal become more familiar with the teacher's learning environment (Zepeda, 1995).

## THE OBSERVATION

There are a variety of data collection techniques available to track classroom events (see, for example, Acheson & Gall, 1997). The data collection techniques in this chapter were developed specifically for some of the instructional techniques presented in Chapter 4 (e.g., cooperative learning and Socratic seminars, transitions between learning activities, and for the beginning and ending of class sessions).

---

### BUILDING BLOCK:
### DIALOGUE IS KEY TO TEACHER
### DEVELOPMENT

Dialogue should be about the teacher and his or her needs. McGreal (1983) indicates that, "the more teachers talk about teaching, the better they get at it."

---

## THE POST-OBSERVATION CONFERENCE

If supervision is viewed as an event, then the post-observation conference will be a nonevent. The post-observation conference, although the last step in the clinical supervision model (and others), is really the beginning for the teacher and the principal. In the post-observation conference:

♦ Data is presented to the teacher for her/his analysis; the teacher should make sense of the data and be prompted into reflecting or thinking through what this information means to his/her practice and to student achievement. Acheson and Gall (1997) refer to this as holding the mirror to the teacher so that the teacher can examine her/his practices based on data within the context of the classroom.

♦ Data, if collected as *just the facts,* will be value-free. Chapter 1 examined Trust-Blocking Responses (Pascarelli & Ponticell, 1994; see Figure 1.4, p. 20) and provided an overview of Reflective Process Tools (Huntress & Jones, 1999; see Figure 1.3, p. 15). You are encouraged to review these figures in addition to the dialogue and feedback sections in that chapter. Zepeda (1999b) reports, in a study of block scheduling, that principals who extended time during the post-observation found, after a while, that "...once teachers did gain confidence,...[some]... were leading conferences with principals instead of just responding" (p. 29) and listening to the principal dominate the post-observation conference. The principals in this study achieved this by "...asking open-ended questions, letting the teacher steer the discussion, [and]...[working] at presenting data from classroom observations in ways teachers can understand" (p. 29).

♦ Extended periods of time are needed so that the events of the classroom can be identified and analyzed. The extended time of the post-observation conference should be proportionate with the time spent in the classroom observation.

## BUILDING SUPERVISORY CAPACITY IN THE BLOCK

Chapter 4 outlines procedures that teachers and principals can use to audit instruction and curriculum. The astute principal audits her/his supervisory climate before proceeding any further as there are several issues that can influence supervision in general, and, more specifically, in the block schedule. Effective principals explore the supervisory landscape before proceeding. Practices that are more likely to promote growth are built jointly by the teacher and the supervisor. Figure 5.2 depicts an audit that will permit effective supervisory practices to be developed based on data relevant to the school site.

---

### FIGURE 5.2. SUPERVISORY FACTORS TO EXAMINE AT THE SITE

---

#### Human Factors

1. Developmental levels of the teachers: Is the teacher in her/his first or fifteenth year of teaching? Are there clusters of entry, mid, and veteran teachers in the building?

2. Number of years in *this* (current) school: How familiar is the teacher with the students in the building? The curriculum? The schoolwide procedures?

3. How much experience does the teacher have teaching in the block?

4. Staff development activities, recency of graduate coursework, or other professional studies.

5. Preparation of the teacher (especially if a recent graduate): Is the teacher traditionally or alternatively certified?

6. Is the teacher an itinerant teacher assigned to two different buildings?

7. Do your teachers know your supervisory style? If you are a first-year or even a veteran supervisor, new to *this* school, your style will, at first, be a mystery to teachers.

#### Organizational Characteristics

1. Where is the school in relation to the block schedule? Has the block schedule been in place for a while or has the block just been implemented?

2. What types of staff development have been offered to teachers prior to and throughout implementing the block schedule?

3. Are there other support systems in the school? Formal and informal mentoring? Induction program for new teachers? Peer coaching teams? Action research teams? Study clusters?

4. What was the supervisory style of the previous supervisor?

5. What has been the history of supervision in the building? Have teachers been supervised or have they been evaluated? Do teachers know the difference between the two processes? What time of the year has supervision typically been conducted (end of the year is evaluation)?

6. In the past, has there been union involvement (grievances) with supervisory or evaluation practices?

7. Do board policies include parameters for supervision? Faculty handbook?

8. If the building is new to the block schedule, have teachers been involved in developing new supervisory and professional development practices?

9. If more than one administrator (e.g., assistant principal, department chair, and district-level curriculum coordinator) is conducting supervision in the building, do they follow the same processes?

---

Information gleaned from reviewing the school's climate regarding supervision and staff development assists the principal in:

♦ Better understanding the school's readiness for examining changes needed to bolster professional development processes;

♦ Anticipating *hot spot* areas (e.g., past grievances) so that discussions and explorations with teachers can be more proactively situated within the context of the school; and,

♦ Steering the course for professional development
toward the needs of teachers while simultaneously
addressing organizational needs.

## DATA COLLECTION INSTRUMENTS
## SUITABLE FOR THE BLOCK

Supervisory decisions based on data will yield more
growth-oriented development. Because block periods range between 90 and 120 minutes, extended classroom observations ne-
cessitate creating new ways of recording classroom events, especially those that provide data for the area(s) identified by the
teacher in the pre-observation conference. For example, if a
teacher wants to know if he/she uses a variety of instructional
methods, the supervisor could track information using the data
collection template presented in Figure 5.3.

## FIGURE 5.3. DATA COLLECTION INSTRUMENT:
## VARIETY OF INSTRUCTIONAL METHODS

Teacher: Mrs. Jones
Course: English I, Unit: Young Adult Literature (*Rumblefish*)
Teacher/Supervisor Focus: Variety of Instructional Methods

| Time | Instructional Method | Teacher Behavior | Student Activities |
|---|---|---|---|
| 9:00–9:15 | Organizing lecture | Lecture, directions for small group work, break students into small groups | Listening, taking notes, asking questions |
| 9:16–9:35 | Cooperative learning | Assist students to get into small groups, passing out materials | Getting into groups, selecting roles (recorder, timer) |
| 9:36–9:50 | | Monitoring student work | Discussing the symbol, the Siamese Fighting fish; finding citations from the text to support ideas |
| 9:51–10:25 | Large group discussion | Leading students to citations offered by groups | Group recorder presenting citations from the text in support of ideas; reading citations offered by other groups |

| 10:26–10:40 | Question and answer | Ask questions | Responding to questions (looking up citations to back up ideas) |
|---|---|---|---|
| 10 41–10:54 | Closure | Assignment given | Asking questions, begin homework assignment |

This same format can be modified if, for example, Mrs. Jones wanted to examine teacher-student discussion with a focus on how student comments are incorporated into the lesson. Figure 5.4 highlights how that data might look.

### FIGURE 5.4. INCORPORATING STUDENT COMMENTS AND IDEAS INTO DISCUSSION

| Time | Teacher Talk | Student Response | Status of Student |
|---|---|---|---|
| 8:50 | A symbol is an object that represents *something else.* What are the symbols in *Rumblefish?* | SR1: Siamese rumblefish SR2: The gangs are made up of people who can't get along with one another. SR3: See page 47. SR4: At the end, the Siamese fighting fish are let go. | Comment Can you expand on this? Cite an example of this from the text? Relate this to the end of the book. Does this parallel the death of the character? |

Supervision can track student responses, and how responses are incorporated into the class discussion. By utilizing a seating chart, the supervisor can also track student-calling patterns.

With extended class periods, multiple instructional techniques and activities are used. Smooth transitions conserve on time, help keep students focused on learning objectives, and reduce opportunities for classroom disruptions. Figures 5.5, 5.6, and 5.7 illustrate data collection templates that might be useful for the supervisor.

### FIGURE 5.5. TRANSITIONS-TRACKING CHART

**Number of Students Present: 27**

| Instruction/ Activity | Transition | Student Response |
|---|---|---|
| 10:00 Getting students into cooperative groups | Directions are given for small cooperative group. Teacher stops movement to give clarifying instructions. | Students meander, finding their group members; 4 students ask clarifying questions during movement. |

### FIGURE 5.6. BEHAVIOR-TRACKING CHART

**Number of Students Present: 27**

| Teacher Behavior | Student Behavior | Notes |
|---|---|---|
| 8:00–8:15 Lecture on author, S. E. Hinton | • Taking notes (4)<br>• Sitting quietly (8)<br>• Reading book (7)<br>• Sidebar discussions (8) | • Advanced organizer?<br>• Theme sheet?<br>• Open up to discussion.<br>• Relate book to S. E. Hinton's life or other books by her or others studied so far? |

## FIGURE 5.7. BEGINNING AND CLOSURE OF
## CLASS SUPERVISION CHART

| Housekeeping Routines Beginning | Housekeeping Routines Closure | Transition to Teaching | Student Behavior |
|---|---|---|---|
| • Attendence<br>• Pass back corrected essays<br>• Announcements from the activities office<br>• Review due dates | • Review my comments on your papers. Revisions are due tomorrow—rewrite only the parts of the essay circled in green | **Direction**<br>• Pull out notebooks and book.<br>**Open-ended Question**<br>• Why is it fitting for the story to end in a pet store? | • 3 students standing in a line in front of the pencil sharpener<br>• 2 students crumple up their essays<br>• students in the back row are getting up and looking for their essays<br>• 3 to 5 students were asking others to borrow pen, paper, book, etc. |

Accurate and value-free classroom data is critical to ensure a more successful post-observation conference. To assist the principal or peer coach, the following tips are offered as a means to handle data collected during an extended period of time:

◆ Record data in small increments of time. It will be easier to work with data in 10- to 15-minute blocks. For example, if an observation lasts 90 minutes, break up the collection into 15-minute segments: 8:00–8:15; 8:15–8:30; 8:30–8:45; 8:45–9:00; 9:00–9:15; and 9:15–9:30;

♦ Utilize seating charts to record data such as calling patterns and teacher movements;

♦ Record major events such as teacher questions and student responses with detail. A few strong examples with complete and accurate information will make more sense than trying to record extraneous information; and,

♦ Leave a space such as a large column in the margin. This space can be utilized during the post-observation conference to make notes (e.g., teacher analysis, questions, concerns, or ideas generated in the post-observation conference).

Often teachers are interested in tracking the types of questions they ask their students. Tracking questions can assist the teacher in analyzing higher-order thinking skills (HOTS). Consider the teacher who identified levels of questions as an instructional focus. The data collection tool in Figure 5.8 focuses the observer on what information to record and is then usable in the post-observation conference to guide the teacher in his/her analysis of the types of questions asked.

In the post-observation conference, the supervisor and teacher will want to explore each level of Bloom's Taxonomy and their attributes:

♦ Knowledge—recalling specific facts;

♦ Comprehension—describing in one's own words;

♦ Application—applying information to produce some result;

♦ Analysis—subdividing something to show how it is put together;

♦ Synthesis—creating a unique, original product; and,

♦ Evaluation—making value decisions about issues. (Bloom, 1956, cited by Orlich, Harder, Callahan, Kauchak, & Gibson, 1994, p. 110)

---

### FIGURE 5.8. QUESTION AND ANSWER
### SEQUENCE TRACKING FORM

---

**Teacher:** Mr. Martin Spain      **Course:** English I

**Unit:** The novel *To Kill a Mockingbird*

**Teacher/Supervisor Focus:** Higher-Order Thinking Skills utilizing Bloom's Taxonomy during a question and answer sequence.

Date _____     Period _____

Time observation began _____     ended_____

**Number of Students present** _____

| Time | Teacher Questions | *Taxonomy Level |
|------|-------------------|-----------------|
| 8:00–8:15 | • What did Jem receive as a Christmas present?<br>• What advice did Atticus give to Jem about this present?<br>• Why did Atticus tell Jem never to kill a mockingbird?<br>• Explain how the mockingbird comes to symbolize innocence, purity, and vulnerability.<br>• How are rabid dogs different from mockingbirds?<br>• Can we relate the stark contrast between killing a mockingbird and a mad dog to any other events in the book? Which ones? How? Why? | |

| Time | Teacher Questions | *Taxonomy Level |
|------|-------------------|-----------------|
| 8:15–8:30 | • Who are the mocking-birds in the book?<br><br>• Give examples of why Tom and Boo are mock-ingbirds.<br><br>• The events of the book and the character of Tom classify him as a mock-ingbird—<br><br>• List the events that sup-port your idea of Tom as a mockingbird.<br><br>• In the end, what new meaning can we attach to the mockingbird? | |

* To be identified by the teacher in the post-observation conference.

Next, the teacher can examine his/her questions and fill in the taxonomy classification for each, discussing how each question fits. The supervisor can assist the teacher to discover any dominant patterns about the ordering of questions. From this information, the teacher and supervisor can look for other dominant patterns such as at what points in the lesson are lower-order or higher-order questions asked and the frequency of each order. The teacher can also chart whether he/she begins a question and answer sequence with a higher-order or a lower-order question.

Throughout the discussion, the supervisor can prompt the teacher to talk about what the question or series of questions was attempting to elicit from student responses. The supervisor can help by:

◆ Encouraging the teacher to reconfigure questions either from higher order to lower order or from lower order to higher order; or,

◆ Demonstrating/modeling, where appropriate, how a question can be reconfigured—always prompting the teacher to *reflect* on the intent of the responses wanted from students.

The key to presenting data rests in the ability of the supervisor to get teachers talking and reflecting on instructional and other classroom practices.

## INFORMAL SUPERVISION AND THE BLOCK: NEW AVENUES FOR TEACHER GROWTH

Supervising teachers is a formative process that is not easily accomplished through the "snapshots" provided by two or three formal observations conducted throughout the year. By augmenting formal observations with informal classroom visitations, a supervisor can construct a more complete picture of the instructional program developing in the classroom. Images of more authentic teacher/student interactions during "live," unrehearsed teaching are, by far, more memorable than the annual dog and pony show put on for the sake of retaining a satisfactory rating.

In addition to informal visits, collegial practices such as peer coaching, auditing, and portfolio development can assist teachers and supervisors to build a continuous "supervisory thread." The "supervisory thread," and the "thread" of staff development embedded in daily tasks are the raw materials from which teachers and supervisors, working alongside each other, weave the "fabric of learning." The durability of this fabric of learning is dependent on building trust between the supervisor and teacher. Blumberg (1980) believes that the lack of trust between teachers and supervisors creates a "private cold war." According to Blumberg:

> At issue is the level of trust between the supervisor and the teacher, which probably bears a direct relationship to the level of threat the teacher perceives in

the situation....Thus, in many cases, the supervisor and the teacher get caught in a degenerative charade that has no real winners. It becomes a tie with the exception that the third and sometimes unwitting party...students...may ultimately lose. (p. 29)

Collaborative forms of supervision can provide the platform for building the trust necessary for establishing authenticity in the learning community.

## INFORMAL CLASSROOM VISITS

Informal classroom visits are short classroom observations not usually connected to formal pre-observation or post-observation conferences. However, the principal can use the information gleaned in an informal observation to provide brief, but specific feedback on what was observed in the window of 5 to 10 minutes. Teachers want context-specific information about their teaching (Zepeda & Ponticell, 1998). Feedback can be as simple as a brief note (card or letter; see Figure 5.9) or as elaborate as a form (see Figure 5.10).

---

### FIGURE 5.9. SAMPLE INFORMAL OBSERVATION NOTE

---

Dear Mary,

I really enjoyed my informal observation on September 3 during your third block Honors English class. The overheads used to illustrate the proper uses of dependent clauses kept students focusing on the common mistakes they made in their own essays.

Clear directions kept students on task when they broke up into small "proofing" groups. The small size of the groups (3) kept *all* students engaged. Perhaps you might want to share these techniques with other freshman Honors teachers!

Thanks, and I hope to see you at the faculty tailgate party tonight!

---

**Figure 5.10. Sample Informal Observation Form**

Teacher _NANCY CANON_____

Date ___12/99_____ Time ___7:45_____ Block __1____

Subject _English_____ Number of students present ___33__

*Students were:*

- ⁻ Working in small, cooperative groups
- ⁻ Making a presentation
- ⁻ Taking a test
- ✗ Working independently at their desks
- ⁻ Viewing a film
- ⁻ Other _____

*Teacher was:*

- ⁻ Lecturing
- ⁻ Facilitating a question and answer sequence
- ✗ Working independently with students
- ⁻ Demonstrating a concept
- ⁻ Introducing a new concept
- ⁻ Reviewing for a test
- ⁻ Coming to closure
- ⁻ Other _____

*Comments:* Nancy:

- ♦ Students were working independently at their desks.
- ♦ The rearrangement of the room (desk, podium, table) allowed you to work independently with students on their essays *and* to keep an eye on students working at their desks.

Perhaps you should hold the next freshman level meeting in your room so others can see your room arrangement.

Thanks for letting me visit your room and see the work you do in order to help our students become better writers. I appreciate your efforts.

*John Dokes*

These visits, also referred to as "pop-ins" (Zepeda, 1995) or "walk-throughs" (Blase & Blase, 1998), provide a way for supervisors keep a "thumb on the pulse" (p. 106), of instructional activity in the school. Informal classroom visits assist supervisors:

♦ To motivate teachers;

♦ To monitor instruction;

♦ To be accessible and provide support; and,

♦ To keep informed [about instruction in the school].
   (Blase & Blase, 1998, pp. 108–109)

Poorly managed informal classroom visitations can be disruptive to the learning environment teachers strive to build. Sergiovanni and Starratt (1998) believe that:

> Successful informal supervision requires that certain expectations be accepted by teachers. Otherwise it [informal supervision] will likely be viewed as a system of informal surveillance. Principals and other supervisors need to be viewed as *principal teachers* who have a responsibility to be a part of all the teaching that takes place in the school. (p. 258, emphasis supplied)

To assist in fostering an environment that supports informal classroom visitations, supervisors need to:

♦ Publish procedures for observations at the beginning of the year;

♦ Schedule informal classroom visits regularly (one or two per week); and,

♦ Track observations. (Zepeda, 1995, p.1)

While poorly organized informal classroom visits can cause feelings of distrust, the lack of a supervisory presence can, for some teachers, create a feeling of abandonment. Blase and Blase (1998) report, from their research, various negative effects on teachers associated with abandonment. Teachers describe:

> ...major adverse effects on *motivation* and *self-esteem*, as well as significant increases in *anger*, *psychic pain*, and feelings of being *unsupported*. Some [teachers]

tried to assuage their sense of abandonment with support from other sources, but many simply tried to avoid their principal altogether....(p. 117, emphasis in the original)

## PEER COACHING AS SUPERVISION

Peer coaching parallels clinical supervision in that it features the pre-observation conference, a credible classroom observation, and a post-observation feedback conference. Pajak (1993) summarizes the elements of peer coaching as supervision:

- *Study*: teachers read about and discuss a particular instructional method or model of teaching;

- *Demonstration*: teachers observe a demonstration of the new method by someone expert in its use;

- *Practice and Feedback*: teachers plan and carry out a lesson featuring the new method with other teachers playing the part of students and receive feedback from colleagues; and,

- *Coaching*: teachers use the new method in the classroom and receive ongoing feedback and support from colleagues. (pp. 211–212)

The cornerstone of professional growth is the "talk" that occurs between professionals. We know, however, that the structures of the school day often diminish opportunities for teachers to talk with one another. It is no surprise then that many teachers just do not know how to talk about teaching since they have not had opportunities to focus discussion on their practices with a trusted colleague, a supervisor, or other adults in the work setting.

Peer coaches, like supervisors, need to ready for a classroom visitation by gathering information about the learners, instructional methods, and a focus so the coach can gather data that will shed light on a particular area of interest for the teacher. Figure 5.11 provides a guide for conducting a peer coaching pre-observation conference. The following form can be tailored to fit either a formal or an informal observation, and moreover, can be tailored to fit the specific needs of either the school's context or the parameters of the peer-coaching program.

## FIGURE 5.11. PEER COACHING PRE-OBSERVATION CONFERENCE FORM

Teacher _____ Coach _____

Pre-observation Conference Date _____ Block _____

Date of Scheduled Observation _____

Anticipated Duration of Classroom Observation _____

### *Learning Context*

Student Characteristics:

♦ Describe your students, including the range of abilities found among learners.

♦ Are there students with unique learning needs (e.g., gifted and talented, special education, other)?

Classroom Climate:

♦ What type of relationships do students have with one another?

♦ How well do students work with one another?

Classroom Culture:

♦ How do students respond to taking risks, experimenting with new ways of learning and to the needs of other learners during group work?

Classroom Context:

♦ Describe how your classroom environment motivates students.

♦ What makes your environment conducive to learning?

Learning Objectives

♦ At the end of the lesson, what do you want your students to have learned? Mastered? Applied?

♦ Given this end view, what are your objectives for the lesson?

*(Figure 5.11 continues on next page)*

- What is the relationship of your objectives to the adopted curriculum?

Instructional Objectives

- What will instruction include? Describe methods:
  - Lecture:
  - Cooperative learning activities:
  - Other activities:
  - Assessment and monitoring strategies:
  - Closure:

Student Involvement Objectives

- During the learning process (regardless of the methods or activities) what should students be doing?
- What will you do to motivate students to participate in the planned activities?
- Are there any students who might need extra attention?
- How will you monitor and assess student involvement?

Materials and resources to be used

- Identify the resources to be used in order to meet objectives (e.g., books, VCR, tapes (audio/video), computer(s), software).
- Are students knowledgeable about the use of materials and resources (e.g., how to boot the computer or how to use the video camera)?

Focus

- *About what aspect of teaching do you feel information could assist you in making more informed decisions (or changes) in your practices?*
- What would you like to examine about either instruction, student activities, interaction patterns, or classroom management? Try to pick one area only for this observation.

♦ Where do you believe the coach should look for this information?

Observation Tools

♦ Based on the focus (identified by the teacher) and the type of information to be collected, the coach should describe how he/she will collect data (what type of data collection instrument (s) will be utilized).

*Date and block period for the post-observation coaching conference*

_____.

The intent of the feedback conference is to get the teacher talking about the events of the classroom. The more the teacher trusts his/her coach, the more authentic the conversation. Several feedback strategies and tips have been offered in this chapter and in Chapter 1. Within the context of a peer coaching post-observation conference, the coach is encouraged to:

♦ Avoid making value judgments;

♦ Encourage the teacher to reconstruct the events of the class period;

♦ Share "written" data in a way that allows the teacher to make sense of it; and,

♦ Use probing questions that are open-ended so that the teacher looks deeply at his/her own practices.

To help the teacher think ahead and to reflect on the possibilities that can be applied from the information discussed in the coaching post-observation conference, the coach can utilize:

♦ *Role Play:* Encourage the teacher to role play a segment of instruction from the lesson. The coach and the teacher can alternate roles (e.g., teacher or student).

♦ *Lesson Reconfiguration in the Block:* The teacher plans out loud how activities, instruction, and classroom procedures would be reconfigured in the block.

♦ *Visualization:* Ask the teacher to talk out what aspects of the lesson could change and how these changes would look. Then ask the teacher to talk out how students might respond to these changes.

Because an increasing number of schools are utilizing peer coaching as an integral part of their overall professional growth program, it is worth identifying the benefits of peer coaching as informal supervision. Peer coaching:

♦ Increases teachers' sense of autonomy by actively taking the lead in their own learning;

♦ Provides teachers with a value-free source of feedback;

♦ Encourages continuous learning for teachers;

♦ Links staff development models such as study groups and problem-based learning with supervision; and,

♦ Furnishes an additional forum for teachers to talk about teaching.

To benefit from coaching, both the coach and the teacher need to make a commitment to continue with follow-up observations. At the end of the coaching post-observation conference, the coach and teacher need to agree upon follow-up activities such as scheduling the next pre-observation conference and classroom visitation. Other follow-up activities might include:

♦ Reading professional articles about a particular teaching method or classroom management procedure;

♦ Engaging in follow-up discussions about experimentation with a teaching method;

♦ Scheduling release time so the teacher can observe one or two teachers use a particular instructional method;

♦ Starting or joining a study or learning cluster group that is exploring a specific concept of interest;

♦ Identifying districtwide or outside staff development activities that would complement the work "under construction" by the teacher; and,

♦ Locating other resources that are available for teachers.

## AUDITING AS SUPERVISION

The intent of supervision is to improve instruction by helping teachers learn about their teaching. If this learning is to occur, teachers need a clear, accurate portrayal of data about *their* teaching. Instructional auditing provides teachers with a mechanism for collecting the data necessary for developing this portrayal.

In Chapter 4, an example concerning a physics teacher demonstrated the use of auditing techniques to collect data (see Figure 4.13, page 111, and accompanying text). A careful examination of the data collected illustrates that many of the problem objectives involved the teacher's use of cooperative learning. This discovery can become a supervisory focus for future classroom observation.

Following the post-observation feedback conference, the teacher, either through coaching, participation in a study group, or self-directed learning, can then repeat the auditing process to help assess progress toward meeting the goal identified as a priority.

## PORTFOLIO DEVELOPMENT AS SUPERVISION

Just as portfolio development can be used to construct and assess student learning, portfolios can also be a valuable tool for facilitating teachers' growth and learning. Portfolios provide a visual record of learning and growth. Portfolios also provide a means for data collection that can lead to action research or to the identification of focus areas for future classroom observations.

Professional portfolios serve many purposes. These include:

♦ Examining one's beliefs and philosophy about teaching and learning;

- Acting as a tool to promote self-analysis and reflection;
- Providing a map of the teacher's professional growth over a period of time;
- Furnishing data for curricular and instructional decision-making;
- Serving as a tool for mentoring new teachers; and,
- Extending information gained from classroom observations and post-observation conferences.

A professional portfolio is a compilation of artifacts that represent the goals, achievements, and professional growth of the teacher. A professional portfolio is, at the same time, both a process and a product; it is always "a work in progress." For the teacher, the portfolio provides a framework for ongoing self-assessment and reflection. For both the teacher and the supervisor, the portfolio provides a frame of reference for the collaborative learning that takes place within an ideal supervisory relationship.

The contents of a professional teaching portfolio might address the following areas:

- Personal (e.g., statement of beliefs concerning teaching, resume, awards, accomplishments);
- Curricular (e.g., sample lesson plans, tests, quizzes, worksheets, and activity guides);
- Classroom (e.g., samples of students work, photos of bulletin boards or other displays, artifacts that demonstrate the use of technology);
- School as a learning community (e.g., interdisciplinary lesson artifacts, extra- and co-curricular activities, committee work, documentation of peer classroom visits); and,
- Professional growth (e.g., career goals, professional growth plan, notes from portfolio discussions, formal observation materials, documentation of completed training or courses, list of resources including web sites, journals, and videotapes).

## VIDEOTAPE ANALYSIS AS SUPERVISION

The advent of user friendly video cameras has provided teachers with an invaluable tool for analyzing their teaching. By videotaping a class period, teachers are able to observe traffic patterns, verbal flow, and activities within the context of their own teaching and classrooms. In other words, teachers now have the option of *autosupervising their own teaching* (Zepeda, Wood, & O'Hair, 1996). While viewing a videotape, teachers can ask themselves these questions:

- Do I achieve my objectives? How?
- What teaching behaviors support the answers to the above questions?
- With the areas that you identified through auto-supervision to study and reflect on, what do you discover about your teaching behaviors? (Zepeda, 1997)

After viewing the videotape, teachers can identify one or two areas or goals for further development and then formulate a plan to realize the desired goals. The teacher should be encouraged to consider videotaping the same class period two or three weeks later to assess progress and to identify areas for further development.

Zepeda (1997) recommends that teachers utilizing videotape analysis think about the following:

- The first videotape could be "unstable." Students might be curious about why a person is in your room videotaping you. Students might divert attention from learning to the camera and the other person in the room. During subsequent videotapings, the novelty should diminish;
- Some people get nervous about the thought of "seeing themselves" live on camera. Teachers might consider viewing the videotape several times to overcome the novelty of the experience;

- After viewing the videotape, recruit a colleague (peer and/or supervisor) to watch the tape and ask for their feedback;
- Recruit a colleague and take turns videotaping and giving feedback to one another; and,
- Include selected videotapes in a professional portfolio. (Zepeda, 1997)

## INFORMAL SUPERVISION AND THE BLOCK

The implementation of a block schedule creates the need for exploring new avenues for professional growth. Teachers will be learning new instructional methods, transitional strategies, and techniques for assessing student learning. Each of these areas of learning provides supervisors with an opportunity to employ diverse supervisory processes to be of assistance to teachers. Specifically, informal supervisory processes can assist supervisors in the block in these ways:

- Informal classroom observations provide a mechanism through which new teaching skills developed for the block (e.g., cooperative learning, transition strategies, student portfolios) may be monitored;
- Peer coaching promotes dialogue between experienced block teachers and novices;
- Videotape analysis allows the teacher to "step outside" the classroom to view his/her teaching. In doing so, the teacher may reflect on progress with new classroom skills (e.g., Socratic seminar, transition strategies);
- Portfolio development allows teachers to build a collection of successful teaching materials (e.g., lesson plans, puzzles used during a transition, hand outs from a simulation); and,
- Auditing can assist teachers learning to vary learning activities within each block period. By tracking content covered and instructional strategies used, both teachers and supervisors can identify, for example, tendencies that might need modification.

Just as the implementation of a block schedule requires teachers to rethink existing practices and to learn new instructional skills, supervisory skills also need to be redesigned. Formal supervision alone cannot support the ongoing professional growth of teachers. Informal practices such as peer coaching, auditing, videotape analysis, and portfolio development help complete the continuum of supervisory support of instruction.

## WORTHWHILE TRENDS TO TRACK IN SUPERVISION AND STAFF DEVELOPMENT

Numerous initiatives for providing staff development, supervision, and evaluation have evolved over the years. With school restructuring and the emergence of the teacher as a professional, this is an exciting time for staff development and supervision. Newer practices to help meet the unique needs of the school community keep emerging; we are entering the millennium of professional enhancement. The following trends are not meant to signal finality; rather, they are presented as a springboard for further consideration. Principals and teachers are encouraged to use their own creativity to discover what will work in their communities.

### TRAILWAYS TO PROFESSIONAL GROWTH

#### *TECHNOLOGY*

With increasing interest, many school systems are moving to incorporate the use of technology into their existing professional development practices. The use of the Internet enables teachers that share common interests to form chat groups via e-mail and specialized servers. Dialogue is continuing on a global basis—teachers can exchange best practices with larger audiences. Colleges and universities are able to *beam up* with teachers from a distance. Technology is a sound tool that can extend professional development; however, it should not supplant or depersonalize staff development or supervision.

Making e-mail available allows more teachers to communicate with one another. Several schools have begun using e-mail as a means of mentoring beginning teachers. Reflection on practice can be enhanced through journaling.

Computerized teaching simulations can be utilized to foster discussion about teaching and learning. The power of CD-ROM and yet-to-be-discovered virtual reality applications will add dimensions to staff development and supervision.

### DEVELOPMENTAL DIFFERENCES NEED TO BE ADDRESSED TO TAILOR PROFESSIONAL GROWTH

The workplace is changing because the profession is grey-ing, because the number of alternatively certified teachers is in-creasing (Chesley, Wood, & Zepeda, 1997), and because the knowledge base about teaching and learning is expanding. Ef-fective principals recognize the developmental ranges of their teachers and professional staff. From a supervisory perspective, needs differ between novice and veteran teachers.

*Novices* need supervisory experiences that:

- ◆ Introduce them to the supervisory process employ-ed by the building and/or district;
- ◆ Engage them in overall goal setting; and,
- ◆ Include supervisory processes such as pre-observa-tion conferences, observations, and post-observa-tion conferences that begin early and continue throughout the year.

*Veteran* teachers need supervisory experiences that:

- ◆ Acknowledge them as professional career teachers who have experiences to draw on as they reflect on their practice;
- ◆ Allow them to develop their own plans for learning and experimentation;
- ◆ Signal to them that risk taking is part of the learning process;
- ◆ Enable professional sense-making; and,
- ◆ Encourage self-assessment and reflection. (Zepeda & Ponticell, 1995)

### EXPANDED ROLES FOR TEACHERS IN DIRECTING THEIR OWN LEARNING

As learning becomes even more central to professional development, teachers will have an expanded role in developing, designing, and facilitating their own learning. According to Ponticell (1995), "teachers are more willing to look at and change classroom practices when they are instrumental in designing and taking charge of their own professional growth activities" (p. 17).

Schools are already beginning to develop new roles for teachers as instructional leaders. In some districts, teachers are recruited and trained as instructional deans with the major responsibility being to supervise and work with teachers on designing professional development opportunities that will enhance classroom performance. The principal and assistant principals remain responsible for evaluating teachers; the instructional deans are responsible for providing more developmentally appropriate assistance that is not remedial in nature.

As schools move into the next millennium, there is a need for principals to continually work at expanding teachers' roles in learning. Teachers who are constantly learning from their own practice and the practices of others, send a powerful message to students—lifelong learning is important.

## IMPLICATIONS

The intent of supervision and staff development must always be to increase gains in student learning while addressing the developmental needs of teachers. Principals can help facilitate teachers' learning in block schedules by:

- Preventing supervision from becoming an isolated, discrete activity;
- Modifying the ways they supervise teachers— longer pre-observations, observations, and post-observations; and,
- Linking needs discovered during the supervisory process to staff development.

## SUMMARY

If principals are to ensure the growth of the professionals who comprise the learning community, then they need to begin thinking of ways to develop and link the growth-oriented activities of the school. This can only be achieved by providing coherence and unity of purpose and by involving those who have the biggest stake in improvement—teachers. A daunting but an achievable task.

## SUGGESTED READINGS

Acheson, K.A., & Gall, M. D. (1997). *Techniques in the clinical supervision of teachers: Preservice and inservice applications* (4th ed.). White Plains, NY: Longman.

Blase, J. R., & Blase, J. (1998). *Handbook of instructional leadership: How really good principals promote teaching and learning.* Thousand Oaks, CA: Corwin Press.

Calabrese, R. L., & Zepeda, S. J. (1997). *The reflective supervisor: A practical guide for educators.* Larchmont, NY: Eye on Education.

Pajak, E. (1993). *Approaches to clinical supervision: Alternatives for improving instruction.* Norwood, MA: Christopher-Gordon.

Zepeda, S. J. (1999b). Arrange time into blocks. *Journal of Staff Development, 20*(2), 26–30.

# 6

# TEACHING IN THE BLOCK: MAINTAINING THE MOMENTUM THROUGH JOB-EMBEDDED STAFF DEVELOPMENT AND SUPERVISION

## CHAPTER OBJECTIVES

> ◆ Identify factors that influence the success of job-embedded learning.
>
> ◆ Describe strategies to embed staff development time into block schedules.
>
> ◆ Highlight staff development and supervisory processes that sustain the momentum for teaching in the block.

Race car drivers spend considerable time and money preparing for each race. Proper preparation provides the driver with the necessary skills, equipment, and support personnel to safely navigate the track. Although advanced preparation is essential, many races are won in the pit. It is the pit crew that helps the driver detect and solve problems *during* the race. The pit crew assists in keeping the driver's momentum going.

The ability of a pit crew to help solve problems during a race is significant for three reasons. First, support from the pit crew does not exist only within the confines of isolated events; it is an ongoing responsibility. Second, assistance from the pit crew is job-embedded; it is an integral part of the race car driver's routine. The driver not only assumes that the pit crew will be there when needed, the driver *depends* on it. Third, the mindset of the pit crew is proactive; they actively search out ways to improve performance to ensure success. A pit crew in action does not necessarily imply that a driver is in trouble, or that there is some problem.

Public schools also have pit crews, better known as staff developers and supervisors. These *mechanics* of the classroom are teachers, principals, and central office administrators. This *pit crew* of staff developers and supervisors is charged with the ongoing responsibility of facilitating and encouraging professional growth. This chapter presents strategies for maintaining the momentum for staff development and supervision once a block schedule is implemented.

## FACTORS THAT INFLUENCE THE
## SUCCESS OF JOB-EMBEDDED LEARNING

Wood and Killian (1998) define job-embedded learning as "learning that occurs as teachers and administrators engage in their daily work activities" (p. 52). Sparks and Hirsh (1997) write that:

> Job-embedded learning...links learning to the immediate and real-life problems faced by teachers and administrators. It is based on the assumption that the most powerful learning is that which occurs in response to challenges currently being faced by the

learner and that allows for immediate application, experimentation, and adaptation on the job. (p. 52)

Job-embedded learning means that staff development and supervision are continuous threads that can be found throughout the culture of a school.

## ATTRIBUTES OF JOB-EMBEDDED LEARNING

Zepeda (1999a) identifies three attributes of successful job-embedded learning: it is relevant to the individual teacher, feedback is built into the process, and it facilitates the transfer of new skills into practice. First, because job-embedded learning is a part of the teacher's daily work, it is, by its very nature, relevant to the learner. Job-embedded learning addresses professional development goals and concerns of the individual teacher. In addition, job-embedded learning occurs *at the teacher's job site.* Therefore, the teacher's learning becomes an integral part of the culture of his/her classroom and school.

Second, through job-embedded learning, feedback is built-in. Zepeda (1999a) describes six processes that can generate feedback: mentoring; peer coaching; reflection and dialogue; study groups; videotape analysis; and journaling. Teachers working in the block can use these tools to chronicle implementation of new instructional skills, to provide artifacts for assessing transition from one learning activity to the next, or to use as material to frame future staff development initiatives. Also, these processes are consistent with more developmental supervisory models (e.g., peer coaching, peer supervision, and videotape analysis of teaching) and processes, such as dialogue, reflection, feedback for refinement of practice, role playing, and simulation.

Third, job-embedded staff development facilitates the transfer of new skills into practice. Research demonstrates that only 10% of teachers are able to transfer newly learned skills into their daily practice. However, when ongoing support through the tools of job-embedded staff development is linked with more responsive forms of instructional supervision, transfer of skills into practice becomes *part of the job.*

## CONDITIONS NEEDED FOR
## JOB-EMBEDDED LEARNING

There are four essential conditions to be met to ensure successful implementation of job-embedded staff development and supervision:

♦ Learning needs to be consistent with the principles of adult learning—learning goals are realistic; learning is relevant to the teacher, and concrete opportunities for practice of skills being learned are afforded;

♦ Trust in the process, in colleagues, and in the learner him/herself must be present—for learning to occur on the job, teachers must be able to trust the process (e.g., peer coaching, videotape analysis), their colleagues, and themselves. Teachers need to know that feedback will be constructive, not personal;

♦ Time within the regular school day needs to be made available for learning—traditionally, staff development takes place after hours, usually at some remote site. Job-embedded learning requires time to be available within the context of the normal working day at the teacher's school site; and

♦ Sufficient resources must be available to support learning—providing release time for teachers' professional development requires the creative use of human resources. Also, outside facilitators are sometimes needed to assist teachers in learning new skills. Funding must be made available to meet these costs. (Zepeda, 1999a)

## BENEFITS OF JOB-EMBEDDED LEARNING

Benefits of quality job-embedded learning are as varied as they are numerous. First, job-embedded learning can, over time, promote collegiality and trust among faculty members. Second, job-embedded learning empowers teachers because the participating teacher(s) are also the design team. Third, job-embedded learning is relevant to teacher's professional responsibilities.

Fourth, principals can multiply themselves by implementing peer supervision. Fifth, job-embedded learning can provide principals time for their own learning.

## BUILDING LEARNING TIME
## INTO BLOCK SCHEDULES

Calabrese and Zepeda (1997) identify the classroom as the heart of the school. Developmentally appropriate supervision and job-embedded staff development are, then, the strands that compose the school's DNA; they are the basic building blocks on which continued growth of the learning community is based. McQuarrie and Wood (1991) believe that "supervision [and] staff development are more than...distinct, independent processes that can be employed to improve instruction. They should...be considered part of a comprehensive approach to improve instructional practices" (p. 94). Growth must be nurtured; it does not occur as a series of discrete, isolated events. Supervision and staff development are the basic building blocks that effective schools use to construct the foundation of a learning organization. Therefore, if consistent growth is to occur on an individual or organizational basis, then time must be appropriated to nurture learning.

Effective principals provide time for teachers to be learners. They also need time to be learners themselves (Zepeda, 1999a). Unfortunately, neither teaching nor administrative schedules are conducive to adult learning. For this reason, time needs to be appropriated during the school year for teachers to be learners. Canady and Rettig (1995) indicate that "teachers need time, not time added onto or squeezed into an already hectic day, but time that is devoted specifically to staff development and personal planning" (p. 183). In addition to days dedicated to adult learning, time within *regular* school days also needs to be made available for teachers.

## EMBEDDING STAFF DEVELOPMENT DAYS
## IN THE SCHOOL YEAR

Tanner, Canady, and Rettig (1995) believe that if principals perceive the available time during the school year as "180 discrete units which can be grouped according to need, the possibilities are increased for developing a multitude of plans," letting learning time be embedded in the school year (p. 16). Time for staff development may be built into the school year by rearranging the schedule within a limited number of school days and then clustering them to form mini-sessions. An example of this type of schedule involves the use of midterm and final sessions.

## USING MIDTERM AND FINAL SESSIONS TO CREATE STAFF DEVELOPMENT TIME

The midterm/final session plan alternates regular 80-day instructional periods with 10-day periods where students are regrouped for special courses while released teachers are involved in professional development. Figure 6.1 depicts the restructured school year using this plan.

Teachers who are released for staff development during the midterm session would assist with student activities during the final session. Teachers assisting with students during the midterm session would then be released for staff development during the final session. Shortening or lengthening the midterm and final sessions may vary this plan. For example, midterm and final sessions could be 5 days each, allowing for 85-day instructional terms.

Building staff development days into the school year by using midterm and final sessions has the advantage of offering teachers time without sending students home. However, it does have the drawback of rearranging and possibly reducing instructional time for students. This can be a politically difficult issue for a district or site to address. For schools using a trimester approach to the accelerated block, the schedule for the school year could be modified as illustrated in Figure 6.2.

In addition to use with the accelerated block, adaptation to the alternating block is possible by inserting the midterm between semesters. Figure 6.3 illustrates the midterm and final sessions embedded in the alternating block.

## FIGURE 6.1. SCHOOL YEAR USING MIDTERM/FINAL SESSIONS (4 x 4 BLOCK)

| Fall Term (80 Days) | Midterm (10 Days) | Spring Term (80 Days) | Final Session (10 Days) |
|---|---|---|---|
| Block 1 | **Student Activities** Electives Community Service | Block 5 | **Student Activities** Electives Community Service |
| Block 2 | Remedial Work Mini-courses Special Programs | Block 6 | Remedial Work Mini-courses Special Programs |
| Block 3 | **Released Teachers** Staff Development: • Peer coaching • Action research • Dialogue • Reflection | Block 7 | **Released Teachers** Staff Development: • Peer coaching • Action research • Dialogue • Reflection |
| Block 4 | | Block 8 | |

Adapted from Tanner, Canady, & Rettig (1995). Scheduling time to maximize staff development opportunities. *Journal of Staff Development, 16*(4), 14–19.

### FIGURE 6.2. SCHOOL YEAR USING
### INTERSESSIONS (TRIMESTERS)

| Trimester 1 (55 Days) | Intersession 1 (5 Days) | Trimester 2 (55 Days) |
|---|---|---|
| Block 1 | **Student Activities**<br><br>Electives<br>Community Service<br>Remedial Work | Block 4 |
| Block 2 | Mini-courses<br>Special Programs<br>**Released Teachers** | Block 5 |
| Block 3 | Staff Development:<br>• Peer coaching<br>• Action research<br>• Dialogue<br>• Reflection | Block 6 |

| Intersession 2 (5 Days) | Trimester 3 (55 Days) | Final Session (5 Days) |
|---|---|---|
| **Student Activities**<br><br>Electives<br>Community Service<br>Remedial Work<br>Mini-courses<br>Special Programs<br><br>**Released Teachers**<br><br>Staff Development:<br>• Peer coaching<br>• Action research<br>• Dialogue<br>• Reflection | Block 7<br><br>Block 8<br><br>Block 9 | **Student Activities**<br><br>Electives<br>Community Service<br>Remedial Work<br>Mini-courses<br>Special Programs<br><br>**Released Teachers**<br><br>Staff Development:<br>• Peer coaching<br>• Action research<br>• Dialogue<br>• Reflection |

FIGURE 6.3. SCHOOL YEAR USING MIDTERM/FINAL SESSIONS (ALTERNATING BLOCK)

| Fall Term (80 Days) | | Midterm (10 Days) | Spring Term (80 Days) | | Final Session (10 Days) |
|---|---|---|---|---|---|
| Block 1 | Block 5 | **Student Activities**<br>Electives<br>Community Service<br>Remedial Work<br>Mini-courses<br>Special Programs<br><br>**Released Teachers**<br>Staff Development:<br>• Peer coaching<br>• Action research<br>• Dialogue<br>• Reflection | Block 1 | Block 5 | **Student Activities**<br>Electives<br>Community Service<br>Remedial Work<br>Mini-courses<br>Special Programs<br><br>**Released Teachers**<br>Staff Development:<br>• Peer coaching<br>• Action research<br>• Dialogue<br>• Reflection |
| Block 2 | Block 6 | | Block 2 | Block 6 | |
| Block 3 | Block 7 | | Block 3 | Block 7 | |
| Block 4 | Block 8 | | Block 4 | Block 8 | |

Making adaptations to the block schedule is complex, but with creativity and planning, time can be manipulated to provide multiple professional development opportunities. Parents and other volunteers can be recruited to assist those teachers who have responsibility for students during the midterm and final sessions. Instructional planning needs to take into account the reduced number of contact days for teachers and students.

---

**BUILDING BLOCK:
STAFF DEVELOPMENT FOR SCHOOL
VOLUNTEERS**

Staff development can be provided for persons who volunteer time to help schools. As a result, volunteers will feel more a part of the team, and will be better prepared for the tasks they are asked to complete.

---

## FACULTY RETREATS

Another strategy for building staff development time into the school year is the use of two-day or three-day periods throughout the school year for faculty retreats. Because it is unrealistic for the entire faculty to attend all of these retreats, this time might be used most effectively for extending planning and learning time for departments or teams. Mathematics teachers could study the use of technology to supplement the existing curriculum or an eleventh grade team could use their retreat for interdisciplinary planning, or a ninth grade team might learn how to implement new variations of cooperative learning in their classrooms.

## BUILDING STAFF DEVELOPMENT TIME INTO THE REGULAR SCHOOL DAY

In addition to building staff development time into the school calendar, time for learning should be regularly built into the routine of school days. The strategies for building periods of extended learning time into the regular school day include:

♦ Rearranging existing time—planning time for teachers is rearranged to create extended time blocks for teacher learning and planning; and,

♦ Creating additional time—planning time, in addition to the traditional daily planning period, is provided for collaborative learning.

How this time is created will depend on what type of schedule has been selected. Schools using the alternating block might need to investigate different options from those who use an accelerated block.

## REARRANGING EXISTING TIME: ROTATING PLANNING DAY

Tanner, Canady, and Rettig (1995) propose the rotating planning day to afford teachers the opportunity to have extended learning or planning time within the confines of regular school days. Particularly well suited for the accelerated block, this plan offers each teacher one full day free of instructional responsibilities every four weeks. Figure 6.4 depicts a four-week rotating planning day schedule.

Advantages of this plan include extended time for collaborative learning and planning. For teachers, the benefits are immense. Teachers could utilize this full day to visit and observe other teachers, attend a conference, or analyze data from audits. Students, too, can benefit from this schedule. Classes that meet for an entire day could use the extended period of time for field trips without student absence from other classes, or for special projects, such as science classes working in an outdoor classroom, or for a drama class that is producing a play. The disadvantage is that teachers must be willing to relinquish their planning period for one day during three of every four weeks.

## CREATING NEW LEARNING TIME

In the best of all worlds, teachers would have extended periods of time for collaborative planning and learning without having to sacrifice any of their traditional planning time. In the

## FIGURE 6.4. FOUR-WEEK ROTATING PLANNING DAY SCHEDULE

| Monday | Tuesday | Wed. #1 | Wed. #2 | Wed. #3 | Wed. #4 | Thursday | Friday |
|---|---|---|---|---|---|---|---|
| Block 1 | Block 1 | Students attend block 1 class all day long | Students attend block 2 class all day long | Students attend block 3 class all day long | Students attend block 4 class all day long | Block 1 | Block 1 |
| Block 2 | Block 2 | Teachers with block 1 planning are released for staff development and planning activities | Teachers with block 2 planning are released for staff development and planning activities | Teachers with block 3 planning are released for staff development and planning activities | Teachers with block 4 planning are released for staff development and planning activities | Block 2 | Block 2 |
| Block 3 | Block 3 | | | | | Block 3 | Block 3 |
| Block 4 | Block 4 | | | | | Block 4 | Block 4 |

Adapted from Tanner, Canady, & Rettig (1995). Scheduling time to maximize staff development opportunities. *Journal of Staff Development, 16*(4), 14–19.

elementary arena, some principals have discovered that by multiplying the school site's manpower through innovative use of outside volunteers, this dream can be realized. The varied and complex nature of the curriculum in the secondary arena creates an ideal setting for enlisting the assistance of outside experts.

Because district and state attendance mandates as well as curricular requirements confine the frequency with which students may be released, schools need to multiply their manpower through volunteers to provide time for teacher learning. The difference between this strategy and the rotating planning day is that instead of regrouping students for instruction by a reduced number of teachers, students are involved in activities such as community service, college programs, career education, or internships with area business or civic groups. The key is the recruitment of enough volunteers to make release of the teaching faculty for a half-day or full day of learning and planning possible.

---

### BUILDING BLOCK:
### SELECTION OF VOLUNTEERS

Schools must be careful in the selection of volunteers. A system through which a volunteer's background can be screened should be a part of the recruitment process.

---

The advantage of this plan is that the entire faculty can be released for learning and planning at the same time. With the entire faculty released, community-building activities that are normally either squeezed into already busy faculty meetings, or that are completely nonexistent, now have a forum. Volunteers to support this effort could come from parents, patrons of the district, and local business and professional people, especially those who look to the local school district to produce the best possible workforce.

# LEARNING MODELS THAT SUSTAIN MOMENTUM FOR TEACHING IN THE BLOCK

Once learning and planning time are built into the school year and into regular school days, district and site staff developers face the decision of how to best utilize these new blocks of time. The remainder of this chapter outlines three models that support ongoing learning: *peer/cognitive coaching, study groups,* and *action research teams.* Each model contains elements of both instructional supervision and staff development; these two processes are, and should be, intertwined.

## PEER/COGNITIVE COACHING

Costa and Garmston (1994) define cognitive coaching as

> ...A nonjudgmental process—built around a planning conference, observation, and a reflecting conference....A coaching relationship may be established between teachers and teachers, administrators and teachers, and/or administrators and fellow administrators. When a cognitive coaching relationship is established between two professionals with similar roles, or *peers*, it can be referred to as peer coaching. (p. 2)

Showers (1985) describe the origins of peer coaching:

> From two unlikely bedfellows—the world of athletics and research on the transfer of training—school districts are borrowing the concept of coaching to increase the effectiveness and acceptability of staff development. (p. 43)

Costa and Garmston identify three purposes of coaching:

♦ Establish and maintain trust;

♦ Facilitate mutual learning; and,

♦ Enhance growth toward *holonomy*...individuals acting *autonomously* while simultaneously acting *interdependently* with the group. (p. 3, emphasis in the original)

Once trust has been established, peer coaching can become supervision without the threat associated with evaluation. The process of coaching mirrors clinical supervision in the sequence of events:

- Pre-observation conference—determining a focus (e.g., study of a new instructional practice, implementation of a new curriculum, or use of a new classroom management system);
- Observation—collection of data to examine behaviors identified in the pre-observation conference; and,
- Post-observation conference—feedback and collaborative problem solving. (Showers, 1985)

Peer coaching is cyclic in nature. Through the feedback and collaborative problem solving during the post-observation, a new focus for the next observation can be formed.

Because there is no evaluation involved, peer coaching provides teachers with a nonthreatening way of having a *second set of eyes*—a colleague who can help facilitate learning through extended dialogue in both the pre-observation and post-observation conferences. Peer coaching provides motivation to study the existing literature on best instructional practice, the impetus to try implementing new practices, and feedback—symbolic of the natural linkage of staff development and instructional supervision.

The formal dialogue that occurs within a coaching relationship underscores the need for informal dialogue. Talking with colleagues about teaching helps break down the isolation created by the confines of classrooms. Informal dialogue also provides a forum completely devoid of value judgments; therefore, teachers are freed to share successes and difficulties in their practices. Open dialogue can be liberating. McGreal (1983) writes, "The benefits of being observed by other teachers and of receiving feedback on one's performance notwithstanding, *the provision for professional dialogue among teachers may be the most telling contribution of colleague consultation*" (p. 129, emphasis supplied).

## STUDY GROUPS

The utilization of study groups is based on the discovery made by Joyce and Showers (1982) that outside experts are no more effective in offering feedback to teachers than teachers themselves. Study groups provide teachers a forum for dialogue, collaborative planning, and team building. According to Murphy (1997), groups should consist of four to six members. Although most study groups are formed across departments or teams, groups can also be homogeneous (e.g., all math or science) in membership.

Makibbin and Sprague (1991) offer three components for successful study groups:

+ A common belief system that supports the need for lifelong learning;
+ Administrative support such as release time and access to research; and,
+ A quality facilitator to keep meetings on track.

Within the context of the block schedule, study groups can provide teachers an ongoing mechanism for *keeping a finger on the pulse* of the school. Effective principals empower teachers to make necessary adjustments in their practices to maintain the momentum of the block schedule. Study groups offer several advantages for schools that have implemented a block schedule. Study groups are:

+ Easily embedded in the block schedule;
+ Comprised of collaborative problem solvers;
+ Supportive of learning in the block; and,
+ Capable of sustaining professional discussion over time.

## ACTION RESEARCH

Marshak (1997) defines action research as:

A methodology through which teachers can formulate a research question that is central to their own professional practice, devise methods of collecting data pertinent to the question, enact the data collection, analyze the data, articulate findings and conclusions that inform their teaching practice, and then change their teaching in ways indicated by the… findings and conclusion. (p. 9)

According to Glanz (1998), there are three major types of action research:

♦ Individual action research: typically conducted by one teacher to investigate a question within his/her classroom;

♦ Collaborative action research: usually conducted within a team or department to investigate a question within a single classroom or one common to several classrooms; and,

♦ Schoolwide action research: normally undertaken by representatives from all stakeholders in the learning community (e.g., administrators, teachers, parents, patrons, community business leaders) to address a schoolwide issue.

Glanz (1998) points out that action research is different from traditional research in three basic ways. According to Glanz, action research is:

♦ Usually less sophisticated or involved;

♦ Normally conducted by practitioners; and,

♦ Generalizable only on a limited basis.

Action research allows practitioners to use research to examine their own professional practice. Because teaching in the block encompasses the use of new instructional and classroom management strategies, action research should become a part of the school site's comprehensive staff development plan. Marshak (1997) identifies the following as possible focal points for action research in the block:

♦ Teacher perception of effective instructional strategies in the block;

- Combinations of instructional strategies that are most effective in the block;
- Student perception of teacher rationale for choosing specific strategies for teaching in the block; and,
- Best use of technology for teaching in the block.

This list is, by no means, exhaustive; it is offered to help the reader to begin exploring possible focal points for her/his own investigations.

Glanz (1998) identifies four steps for conducting action research:

- Select a focus—decide what you want to investigate and what questions will help elicit the information needed; then design a plan to answer those questions;
- Collect data—gather information, using such tools as Likert scale instruments, observations, interviews, criterion-referenced and norm-referenced tests, discussion/focus groups, school profile data (e.g., attendance statistics, discipline referrals), or portfolios;
- Analyze and interpret data—use statistical tests on quantitative data, develop themes in qualitative data; and,
- Take action—develop a plan of action based on the information collected and analyzed. (pp. 24–26)

According to Marshak (1997), the connection between action research and the block schedule is "a natural one" (p. 23):

Collaborative action research gives teachers a method through which they can explore the uses of block-period structures and develop and refine both these new structures and their teaching practice within these contexts. Collaborative action research is a way of discovering how to teach more effectively for the purpose of generating student learning and growth, how to implement innovation, and how to demonstrate the validity of both innovations and

fruitful traditional methods to colleagues, administrators, parents, and the public at large. (p. 24)

Learning that results from action research in one focus area
often leads to new avenues for further investigation. Schools in
which action research is an integral part of staff development,
realize the power of action research—data informs practice.
Glickman, Gordon, and Ross-Gordon (1998) describe the powerful effect of action research on supervision and staff development:

> Think of action research as a huge meteor falling into
> the middle of the supervision ocean. As it hits, it
> causes a rippling of water.... The rippling of water
> continues to increase in force until a giant wave gath-
> ers and crashes onto all instructional shores, sweep-
> ing away the old sand of past instructional failures
> and replacing it with the new sand of instructional
> improvement. (p. 412)

Action research can act as a fulcrum for professional growth
by purposefully uniting supervision and staff development.
Each school is unique; therefore, principals are encouraged to
unite the processes of supervision and staff development that
make sense to their setting. By linking efforts, practices—action
research, supervision, and staff development—can become embedded within the organization. The results are profound for
adults—learning becomes a seamless *habit of practice*.

## IMPLICATIONS

*One-shot* staff development is woefully inadequate for supporting teachers' learning needs. Achieving optimal student
learning in the block schedule requires teacher learning to be
ongoing. Therefore, principals need to support staff development and supervision that is job-embedded. To this end, a baseline of support includes:

   ♦ Release time for study groups, workshops, and re-
     flection; and,

♦ Supervision that promotes innovation and risk-taking in teacher's classroom practices.

## SUMMARY

Learning expends resources. In addition to staff development conducted outside of school hours, teachers need learning opportunities that are a part of their daily work. Fulfilling this need requires time. Providing learning resources for the school's most important human resource—teachers—is critical. Principals make lasting investments in learning for both teachers and students by providing time for professional development.

Sustaining the impetus for teacher growth once a block schedule is in place requires the diligence and skill of a pit crew of master mechanics. Staff development mechanics are planners, problem solvers, coaches, and cheerleaders. Through job-embedded learning techniques such as coaching, study groups, and action research, these mechanics can assist teachers to refine their practices to maintain the momentum.

## SUGGESTED READINGS

Marshak, D. (1997). *Action research on block scheduling.* Larchmont, NY: Eye on Education.

Sparks, D., & Hirsh, S. (1997). *A new vision for staff development.* Oxford, OH: National Staff Development Council.

Tanner, B., Canady, R. L., & Rettig, M. D. (1995). Scheduling time to maximize staff development opportunities. *Journal of Staff Development, 16*(4), 14–19.

Wood, F. H., & Killian, J. (1998). Job-embedded learning makes the difference in school improvement. *Journal of Staff Development, 19*(1), 52–54.

Zepeda, S. J. (1999a). *Staff development: Practices that promote leadership in learning communities.* Larchmont, NY: Eye on Education.

# 7

# EVALUATING THE BLOCK SCHEDULE

*Judith A. Ponticell*[*]
*Arturo Olivarez*

## CHAPTER OBJECTIVES

- ◆ Define different types of program evaluation.
- ◆ Present steps to organizing an evaluation.
- ◆ Identify key features of an evaluation report.
- ◆ Differentiate between *doing* an evaluation and *using* an evaluation.

---

[*] *Judith Ponticell* is an associate professor in the Division of Educational Leadership and Organizational Learning at the University of New Mexico. *Arturo Olivarez* is an associate professor in Educational Psychology and Leadership at Texas Tech University. They have guided or conducted over 80 evaluations of school, district, university, and corporate programs.

Why is a chapter on evaluating a block schedule included in this book? Schools today face challenges. To address these challenges, schools and districts launch programs intended to resolve problems, improve conditions, and get results. Sometimes programs are *judged* to be ineffective and scrapped. All too often such judgments are based on perceptions alone rather than on systematically collected evidence, examined in relation to specific, intended goals.

Educators and policy makers need to make good decisions. To make intelligent choices, educators and policy makers need good information. What programs are working? Which are not working well and why? What intended results have been realized? Which have not? Which parts of programs have been contributing more than others? Which parts are not contributing and why? What staff development is needed? What changes in supervision are needed? What monitoring is needed? In which areas do programs need to be improved? Are there parts of programs or entire programs that should be discontinued? Finding answers to questions such as these is the task of *program evaluation, the task of judging the worth or merit of a program* (Scriven, 1967).

From the information collected, decision-makers can make more informed decisions about retaining or abandoning a program. They can also determine specific staff development needs and select training and development activities targeted toward program improvement.

## DEFINE DIFFERENT TYPES OF PROGRAM EVALUATION

### FORMATIVE AND SUMMATIVE PROGRAM EVALUATION

Both formative and summative evaluation are important. Decisions are needed during the day-to-day operation of a block schedule to strengthen and improve it. Decisions are also needed to judge the final worth of a block schedule and to determine its continuation, revision, or termination.

## FORMATIVE EVALUATION

*Formative evaluation* of a block schedule can provide teachers and administrators with information useful in modifying and improving the schedule as it is implemented on a day-to-day basis. A formative evaluation can determine which goals are not being achieved to their desired level. For example, teachers in the mathematics department might examine the characteristics of students who appear not to do well in mathematics in the block schedule and identify reasons for their lower performance (e.g., What other courses are students taking? What time of day are the mathematics courses offered? What is the content of the curriculum being taught? Have there been gaps in students' mathematics sequence because courses were not offered to allow students to take mathematics in contiguous semesters? What teaching strategies are being used in mathematics courses?). Armed with answers to questions such as these, teachers might explore ways to modify the schedule, the content of the curriculum, or the instructional strategies they use. Supervision and staff development activities can be selected based on teachers' improved understanding of the students and their needs.

## SUMMATIVE EVALUATION

*Summative evaluation* of a block schedule would provide decision-makers and consumers with judgments about the schedule's worth or merit, particularly in relation to intended results. For example, suppose a block schedule was intended to improve students' performance in mathematics on standardized achievement tests. A summative evaluation might compare current students' performance in mathematics on a state or district standardized test to trends in performance of previous students before the implementation of the block schedule. If the block schedule is having the intended effect on students' mathematics performance, the scores of current students should be higher than the trend in the scores of previous students. If the block schedule is having no effect, the mathematics scores of current students should be approximately the same as the trend in the scores of previous students. If the block schedule is having a negative effect, the mathematics scores of current students should be significantly lower than the trend in the scores of previous students.

## DIFFERENCES BETWEEN FORMATIVE AND SUMMATIVE EVALUATION

The important differences between formative and summative evaluation lie in the purposes and audiences for which they are conducted. In formative evaluation, the audience is the teachers, staff, and administrators responsible for the day-to-day implementation of the block schedule program. Formative evaluation leads to decisions about timely modification and improvement, and identifies learning needs. In summative evaluation, the audience is also teachers, staff, and administrators, but expands to decision-makers and consumers. Summative evaluation leads to decisions about the continuation, revision, or termination of the block schedule program.

Unfortunately, too often in schools and school districts, only summative evaluation is done, and it is done sporadically. For example, a block schedule might be put in place and run for five years before anyone systematically examines its effectiveness. Then, once such a summative evaluation is conducted, the tendency is to conduct no other evaluations to confirm the retained effectiveness of the program.

## INTERNAL VS. EXTERNAL EVALUATION

An *internal evaluation* is an evaluation conducted by the teachers, staff, and administrators who work in the block schedule program. Outsiders conduct an *external evaluation*. Both types of evaluation have their advantages.

### INTERNAL EVALUATION

Internal evaluators most often conduct a formative evaluation of a block schedule. Internal evaluators are likely to know more about the block schedule and its history. They are more familiar with information sources and consumers. Internal evaluators also know more about the history of the school or district and about the typical decision-making processes used. This knowledge allows internal evaluators to work as advocates after the evaluation to persuade teachers, staff, and administrators to use evaluation findings to improve the block schedule program. Also, program teachers, staff, and administrators know internal evaluators. The internal evaluator's strengths and weaknesses are also known, so decisions about task assignments may be easier.

Internal evaluators, however, may be so close to the block schedule program that they are unable to be objective about the information they collect and interpret. This can be both a disadvantage and an advantage. Worthen, Sanders, and Fitzpatrick (1997) note:

> One often finds an internal evaluator who is full of unimportant details about the program but overlooks several critical variables.... On the other hand, the internal evaluator is much more likely to be familiar with important contextual information (for example, the serious illness of the director's husband, which is adversely affecting the director's work) that would temper evaluation recommendations. (pp. 18–19)

Although internal evaluators may lack complete objectivity, the purpose of formative evaluation is the gathering of information to guide the improvement of the block schedule as it is implemented on a day-to-day basis. So, internal evaluators' potential lack of objectivity may not matter in relation to the insights these insiders can provide.

## EXTERNAL EVALUATION

External evaluators should conduct summative evaluation of a block schedule. Here, objectivity is important in the interpretation of information that will be used for making decisions about the continuation, revision, or termination of the block schedule. External evaluators would have distance from the planning and implementation of the block schedule, so they would be likely to be more impartial in the entire evaluation process. They are also likely to be more credible to audiences outside the day-to-day operation of the block schedule. This can be of particular advantage when the evaluation of the block schedule takes place in a context or political climate of controversy or dispute. To this, external evaluators can bring fresh, outside perspectives. External evaluators are also likely to have less concern about presenting unpopular information. They are less likely to breach confidentiality, as they have no continuous contact on-site after the evaluation ends.

### INTERNAL OR EXTERNAL?

Both internal and external evaluations have their place, and they are not mutually exclusive. For example, where financial constraints or unavailability of expert external help are problems, choosing internal evaluators who have at least some distance from the actual development and delivery of the block schedule (e.g., teachers, staff, or administrators from another school, or central office personnel) may allow a school or district to retain some semblance of objectivity and credibility. External evaluators might then be used to audit the evaluation report, confirming for various audiences the credibility of the conduct of the evaluation, the findings, and the recommendations (Chen, 1994).

External evaluators can also work with internal evaluators who collect much of the necessary information and communicate results and recommendations to different audiences. The school or district can save travel money if the external evaluator is on-site only to conduct key tasks where sensitive information or possible bias is involved.

### SELECTING AN EXTERNAL EVALUATOR

Choosing an external evaluator is an important task. Sanders (1979) suggests that external evaluators should have several key abilities. These include:

♦ Working with different audiences to identify key evaluation questions and demonstrating sensitivity to the needs of program teachers, staff, and administrators; decision-makers; and consumers;

♦ Communicating clearly what is being evaluated and why;

♦ Conceptualizing the evaluation design, identifying appropriate information sources, skillfully conducting data collection, analysis, and interpretation of findings;

♦ Employing cost effective planning and management of evaluation tasks;

♦ Communicating environmental factors affecting the block schedule and the evaluation;

♦ Communicating evaluation findings clearly to different audiences;

♦ Preparing judgments and recommendations based on systematic, justifiable findings; and,

♦ Demonstrating an ethical and confidential working manner.

### INFORMATION TO REQUEST

What do you request of an external evaluator when considering the individual for an evaluation?

♦ A résumé that describes the individual's training and past experiences with program evaluation;

♦ Past evaluation reports, so that you can judge the individual's expertise in writing a high utility report;

♦ An interview, so that you can assess the individual's interest in the block schedule program, communication skills, sensitivity to and ability to interact with different audiences, ability to explain complex issues clearly, and ability to listen and learn about your needs and concerns; and,

♦ Former clients, so that you can talk with schools and districts who have used this evaluator to conduct a program evaluation for them. A conversation about their experiences should help you discover the positive and negative aspects of the evaluator's conduct.

## GETTING STARTED

*Understanding what prompts an evaluation is important* (Worthen, Sanders, & Fitzpatrick, 1997). An evaluation is generally initiated because someone wants to know something. Both the school and district initiating the evaluation and the evaluators need to know what motivates an evaluation.

### KEY QUESTIONS

- ◆ Why is the evaluation being initiated? What questions is it intended to answer?

- ◆ Who will use the evaluation findings and recommendations, and for what purpose? Who additionally needs to be informed?

- ◆ How much time and money are available for the evaluation? Is some information needed more urgently than other information? Who is available to do the evaluation? Will the evaluators be internal or external? What is the timeline for completing the evaluation?

- ◆ What are the essential goals of the block schedule? What are the essential activities involved in its day-to-day implementation? What will be included in the evaluation, and what will not be included? Why?

- ◆ Who will be the key communicators and information sources?

- ◆ Has the block schedule been evaluated before? When? By whom? For what purpose? Are the evaluation findings and recommendations available? How were the evaluation findings and recommendations used?

- ◆ What is the context and political climate surrounding the evaluation of the block schedule? Are there aspects of the context and political climate that might interfere with the conduct of a fair and meaningful evaluation?

The point of questions such as these is that they will help the school or district and the evaluators to identify information needs and perceptions surrounding the evaluation. Insights gained will be important to determining appropriate evaluation activities and to the utility of the evaluation.

## COMMITTING RESOURCES TO THE EVALUATION

A common concern about conducting a program evaluation is that resources committed to the evaluation are resources taken away from the program itself. In the case of an evaluation of a block schedule, various audiences may complain, "That money could be used for the students!" If a school or district recognizes that the purpose of formative evaluation is to improve the quality and effectiveness of the block schedule and that the purpose of summative evaluation is to determine whether the block schedule has delivered intended results, then students will benefit.

### BASIC CONSIDERATIONS FOR A
### COST-FEASIBLE EVALUATION

What should a school or district consider for a cost-feasible evaluation? If there is a limit to the funds the school or district can expend for an evaluation, say so! Don't lead evaluators to think there is more money available than there is. Ask the evaluators to propose two or three levels of evaluation that differ in cost and comprehensiveness, so that you can select the evaluation design that meets your needs in terms of both information and finances.

An external evaluator can work with an internal evaluator to reduce costs. Program staff may be able to collect much of the necessary information. Secretaries or administrative assistants can search for records. Graduate students from nearby universities who want internship experiences in program evaluation can collect data and enter data (e.g., survey and interview responses). Parents or community volunteers can perform nontechnical tasks such as photocopying records and other information or setting up survey packets.

**BUILDING BLOCK:
A WORD OF CAUTION**

When individuals who are not evaluation specialists assist with evaluation tasks, evaluators must orient these individuals to the purpose of the evaluation and the role that the individuals are being asked to play. They must train the individuals in the skills they will need to perform their tasks, and they will have to monitor the tasks performed.

## PRODUCING AN EVALUATION REPORT

### IDENTIFYING AUDIENCES

Because an evaluation ends in some type of report, it is important for evaluators to know the audiences for the report and how the report is to be used by each audience. Guba and Lincoln (1981) developed a set of questions to assist the evaluator in identifying potential audiences:

- Which audience is involved in supporting or developing the program to be evaluated?
- Which audience potentially benefits from the program?
- Which audience may see the program as a disadvantage?

### COMMON AUDIENCES

- The developer(s) of the program;
- The funder(s) of the program;
- Boards/agencies which approved the program;
- Administrators, teachers, and staff managing and/or delivering the program;
- Consumers of the program;

- Groups perceiving negative effects of the program; and,
- General school public/community.

## USES FOR THE EVALUATION REPORT

All audiences are not interested in the same information. Some common uses for the evaluation report are:

- To make policy;
- To make continuation or termination decisions;
- To make operational decisions;
- To provide input into the evaluation;
- To react to the evaluation report; and,
- To receive general information about the program.

Worthen and Sanders (1987) remind us that any one evaluation would generally not have all the audiences listed, nor serve all the uses for the evaluation report. But it is important for evaluators to talk with key communicators who represent various audiences to learn what they perceive as the purpose of the program to be evaluated, how well they think it works, their concerns about the program, what they have heard about the evaluation, what they hope to learn from the evaluation, and their concerns about the evaluation. Important audiences might be involved in an evaluation advisory group, in data collection and interpretation of results, or as information sources. Some audiences will have little or no interest in participating in the evaluation process itself.

## GENERATING A PROGRAM DESCRIPTION

A clear description of the block schedule program establishes the context of the evaluation. A program description does not have to be long, but it must be detailed enough to provide a foundation for the program evaluation and a common understanding of the program for the audiences. Components of a good description of a block schedule program include:

- Information about the problem(s) the block schedule was intended to address or the need(s) the block schedule serves, why the block schedule was initiated, its goals, and its intended beneficiaries;

♦ The basic structure of the block schedule, its major components and activities;

♦ The history of the block schedule; and,

♦ Previous evaluation information, findings, and recommendations.

How do program evaluators develop the program description? Evaluators can read information documents about the block schedule, talk with key communicators familiar with the program, and/or observe the block schedule in action.

## IDENTIFYING AND SELECTING EVALUATION QUESTIONS

Program evaluations are designed to answer questions. Questions direct the evaluation. Questions can come from many sources. Probably the most important sources are the program's participants and the audiences for the evaluation report. Common sources of questions, insights, perceptions, hopes, or concerns are:

♦ Policy makers (e.g., school board members);

♦ Administrators and/or program managers;

♦ Practitioners who deliver the program;

♦ Consumers (e.g., students, parents); and,

♦ Audiences (e.g., citizens, community groups).

To ascertain evaluation questions, evaluators most commonly interview these sources to determine:

♦ Their general perceptions of the program;

♦ Their concerns;

♦ What they see as the major goals and results of the program;

♦ What program activities they see leading to these goals and results;

- What activities they see as critical to achieving these goals and results;
- What program activities they see as negatively affecting the attainment of these goals and results; and,
- What they would do with the program evaluation findings.

Worthen, Sanders, and Fitzpatrick (1997) suggest several criteria for determining which questions suggested by the evaluators' sources are appropriate to guide the evaluation:

- Will the question be of interest to key audiences?
- Will the answer reduce uncertainty? Does the answer already exist?
- Would the answer yield important information?
- Is the question merely of passing interest to one individual, or is it of lasting interest to many?
- If the question were dropped, would the comprehensiveness of the evaluation be limited?
- Will the answer have an impact on decision making?
- Can the question be answered within available financial and human resources, time, methods, and technology?

Figures 7.1 and 7.2 present a sample of useful key questions for quantitative or qualitative analysis in the evaluation of a block schedule.

## FIGURE 7.1. SAMPLE OF USEFUL KEY QUESTIONS FOR QUANTITATIVE ANALYSIS

| Key Areas of Concern | Key Evaluation Question |
|---|---|
| | For each of the 3 to 5 years prior to the implementation of the block schedule and for each year since the implementation of the block schedule... |
| National Standardized Test Performance | What trends are seen in both overall and demographic group performance on national standardized tests such as the ACT, SAT, and/or PSAT? What trends were seen in national performance in the same demographic groups? What was the number of National Merit finalists, semi-finalists, and commendations? |
| State Standardized Achievement Test Performance | What trends are seen in both overall and demographic group performance in key content areas (e.g., reading, language arts, mathematics) of state standardized achievement tests? What trends were seen in statewide performance in the same demographic groups? |
| Advanced Placement Test Results | What percentage of Advanced Placement students, both overall and by demographic group, scored a 3 or better on AP tests? What trends were seen in statewide performance in the same demographic groups? What trends were seen in national performance in the same demographic groups? |
| Students' Grades | What trends are seen in students' grades on final examinations, semester grades, and/or final course grades (i.e., number of A's, B's, C's, D's, F's)? |

| Key Areas of Concern | Key Evaluation Question |
|---|---|
| | *For each of the 3 to 5 years prior to the implementation of the block schedule and for each year since the implementation of the block schedule…* |
| Attendance | What trends are seen in the average yearly attendance? |
| Failure Rates | What percentages of students, both overall and by demographic group, failed at the semester and end of the year in core subject areas (e.g., English/language arts, mathematics, science, social studies)? |
| Graduation Failure Rates | What number of students, both overall and by demographic group, failed to graduate? |
| Dropout Rates | What number of students, both overall and by demographic group, dropped out of school? |
| Discipline | What number of students, both overall and by demographic group, are referred to administrative offices for disciplinary reasons? |
| Suspensions | What number of students, both overall and by demographic group, are suspended from school (indicate in-school and out-of-school suspensions separately)? |
| Personnel | What trends are evident in teacher hiring, retirements, and transfers? |
| Facilities | What trends are evident in the percentage of use of classrooms for academic classes (i.e., the percentage of time during the day that classrooms are scheduled for courses)? |

**FIGURE 7.2. SAMPLE OF USEFUL KEY QUESTIONS**
**FOR QUANTITATIVE OR QUALITATIVE ANALYSIS**

| *Key Areas of Concern* | *Key Evaluation Question* |
|---|---|
| Learning | What percentage of students, teachers, and parents perceive that students are able to learn better in the block schedule? |
| Time Management | What percentage of students, teachers, and parents perceive that students are better able to manage their time in the block schedule? |
| Teaching Strategies | What percentage of students, teachers, and parents perceive that teachers are using a variety of teaching strategies during class periods in the block schedule? |
| Curriculum Content | What percentage of students, teachers, and parents perceive that teachers are able to cover enough course content in the block schedule? |
| Retention of Concepts | What percentage of students, teachers, and parents perceive that students are able to remember key concepts from one course to the next level of course work in the same content area? |
| Pacing | What percentage of students, teachers, and parents perceive that content is presented too quickly for students to understand? |
| Teacher Availability | What percentage of students, teachers, and parents perceive that students receive more individual assistance from teachers in the block schedule? |

| *Key Areas of Concern* | *Key Evaluation Question* |
|---|---|
| Length of Class Period | What percentage of students, teachers, and parents are satisfied with the length of the class periods in the block schedule? |
| Completion of Class Work | What percentage of students, teachers, and parents perceive that students are able to complete their work in the block schedule? |
| Impact of Absenteeism on Class Work | What percentage of students, teachers, and parents perceive that student absenteeism negatively affects the completion of class work? |
| Availability of Electives | What percentage of students, teachers, and parents perceive that students have sufficient choices in electives available to them in the block schedule? |
| Availability of Advanced Courses | What percentage of students, teachers, and parents perceive that students have sufficient advanced courses available to them in the block schedule? |

It is important to remember that intervening events, changes in personnel or in the focus of an evaluation, or new information can require changing the evaluation questions that are asked. Evaluators must be flexible and open to new or revised evaluation questions. But, evaluators must also remain focused on the purpose of the evaluation. Resources should not be redirected from the evaluation's key purpose to pursue new issues just because they are interesting!

## IDENTIFYING DATA COLLECTION AND ANALYSIS METHODS

Evaluation questions guide what information is needed to answer each question. Evaluators should involve those requesting the evaluation in determining what information would best answer each evaluation question.

Common information sources include:

- Existing reports or information collected for other reasons (e.g., files, status reports, previous evaluation reports, performance reports, minutes of meetings);
- Public documents and data bases (e.g., census reports, federal or local agency reports);
- Surveys, questionnaires, and inventories;
- Interviews;
- Focus groups;
- Journals or logs;
- Work samples (e.g., products made by students, teachers, or other employees); and,
- Videotapes or photographs.

Figure 7.3 provides a sample of possible information sources for the evaluation questions presented in Figures 7.1 and 7.2.

**FIGURE 7.3. POSSIBLE INFORMATION SOURCES FOR KEY QUESTIONS PRESENTED IN FIGURES 7.1 AND 7.2**

| Key Questions | Information Source |
|---|---|
| What trends are seen in both overall and demographic group performance on national standardized tests such as the ACT, SAT, and/or PSAT? What trends were seen in national performance in the same demographic groups? What was the number of National Merit finalists, semi-finalists, and commendations? | ACT, SAT, and/or PSAT Score Reports<br><br>National Merit Scholar Reports |
| What trends are seen in both overall and demographic group performance in key content areas (e.g., reading, language arts, mathematics) of state standardized achievement tests? What trends were seen in statewide performance in the same demographic groups? | State Score Reports |
| What percentage of Advanced Placement students, both overall and by demographic group, scored a 3 or better on AP tests? What trends were seen in statewide performance in the same demographic groups? What trends were seen in national performance in the same demographic groups? | Advanced Placement Test Reports |
| What trends are seen in students' grades on final examinations, semester grades, and/or final course grades (i.e., number of A's, B's, C's, D's, F's)? | School and/or District Grade Summaries |

| Key Questions | Information Source |
|---|---|
| What trends are seen in the average yearly attendance rates? | School and/or District Attendance Reports |
| What percentages of students, both overall and by demographic group, failed at the semester and end of the year in core subject areas (e.g., English/language arts, mathematics, science, social studies)? | School and/or District Course Failure Reports |
| What number of students, both overall and by demographic group, failed to graduate? | School and/or District Graduation Failure Reports |
| What number of students, both overall and by demographic group, dropped out of school? | School and/or District Drop Out Reports |
| What number of students, both overall and by demographic group, are referred to administrative offices for disciplinary reasons? | School and/or District Discipline Referral Reports |
| What number of students, both overall and by demographic group, are suspended from school (indicate in-school and out-of-school suspensions separately)? | School and/or District Suspension Reports |
| What trends are evident in teacher hiring, retirements, and transfers? | School and/or District Personnel Reports |

| *Key Questions* | *Information Source* |
| --- | --- |
| What trends are evident in the percentage of use of classrooms for academic classes (i.e., the percentage of time during the day that classrooms are scheduled for courses)? | School and/or District Facilities Usage Reports |
| What percentage of students, teachers, and parents perceive that students are able to learn better in the block schedule? | Survey, Structured Interview |
| What percentage of students, teachers, and parents perceive that students are better able to manage their time in the block schedule? | Survey, Structured Interview |
| What percentage of students, teachers, and parents perceive that teachers are using a variety of teaching strategies during class periods in the block schedule? | Survey, Structured Interview, Observation |
| What percentage of students, teachers, and parents perceive that teachers are able to cover enough course content in the block schedule? | Survey, Structured Interview, Curriculum Mapping |
| What percentage of students, teachers, and parents perceive that students are able to remember key concepts from one course to the next level of course work in the same content area? | Survey, Structured Interview, Pre-test of Key Concepts in Next Level Courses |
| What percentage of students, teachers, and parents perceive that content is presented too quickly for students to understand? | Survey, Structured Interview, Curriculum Mapping |

| Key Questions | Information Source |
|---|---|
| What percentage of students, teachers, and parents perceive that students receive more individual assistance from teachers in the block schedule? | Survey, Structured Interview |
| What percentage of students, teachers, and parents are satisfied with the length of the class periods in the block schedule? | Survey, Structured Interview |
| What percentage of students, teachers, and parents perceive that students are able to complete their class work in the block schedule? | Survey, Structured Interview, Review of Teachers' Grade Books |
| What percentage of students, teachers, and parents perceive that student absenteeism negatively affects the completion of class work? | Survey, Structured Interview |
| What percentage of students, teachers, and parents perceive that students have sufficient choices in electives available to them in the block schedule? | Survey, Structured Interview, Course Mapping |
| What percentage of students, teachers, and parents perceive that students have sufficient advanced courses available to them in the block schedule? | Survey, Structured Interview, Course Mapping |

---

**BUILDING BLOCK:**
**SECURING PERMISSION**
**TO COLLECT DATA**

Be sure that you consult school or district policies regarding the collection of information. There
may be restrictions on employee or consumer participation in data collection or on accessibility of files
or documents. Parental or guardian permission
may be needed before information can be obtained
from students.

---

It is important to determine who will collect the information, what training is needed to ensure that data collection proceeds appropriately, where data collection will occur and when,
what equipment or materials are needed, and how anonymity
and confidentiality will be protected. For each evaluation question, evaluators should also specify how the collected information is to be analyzed (i.e., what statistical or summary techniques will be used?).

Figure 7.4 presents a useful matrix for planning which information sources to use for which evaluation questions, data to be
collected, personnel responsible, data analysis methods, and audiences for the findings.

## FIGURE 7.4. EVALUATION PLANNING MATRIX

| Evaluation Question | Information Source | Data Collection Method and Due Date | Personnel Responsible | Data Analysis Method and Due Date | Audience for Findings |
|---|---|---|---|---|---|
|  |  |  |  |  |  |

## PREPARING THE EVALUATION REPORT

The basic function of the evaluation report is to inform appropriate audiences of the findings and conclusions resulting from the collection, analysis, and interpretation of information gathered to answer the evaluation questions. Evaluation reports can serve many purposes, depending upon the role that the evaluation is intended to play. Brinkerhoff, Brethower, Hluchyj, and Nowakowski (1983) list nine purposes that can be served by evaluation reports:

+ Demonstrate accountability;
+ Convince;
+ Educate;
+ Explore and investigate;
+ Document;
+ Involve;
+ Gain support;
+ Promote understanding; and,
+ Promote public relations.

## IDENTIFY THE AUDIENCE

A good evaluation report begins with a clear identification of its audience(s) and the potential questions or responses of that audience to the evaluation findings and conclusions. The evaluation report must be tailored to the language and level of sophistication of the audience, so that evaluation findings and conclusions can be clearly understood. Cousins and Leithwood (1986) found that a combination of oral and written reports, delivered in nontechnical language, had a higher impact on the evaluation's audience(s).

## WRITE THE REPORT

Worthen, Sanders, and Fitzpatrick (1997) indicate that there are some important items that should be included in almost every evaluation report. They offer a generic table of contents (pp. 414–415) that we find very useful and have modified for a report regarding a block schedule evaluation (see Figure 7.5).

One critical feature of the evaluation report is balanced reporting. The Joint Committee on Standards for Educational Evaluation (1994) states, "The evaluation should be complete and fair in its presentation and recording of strengths and weaknesses of the program being evaluated, so that strengths can be built upon and problem areas addressed" (p. 105).

Another critical feature of the evaluation report is clear communication. Worthen, Sanders, and Fitzpatrick (1997) suggest several *rules* for clear communication in evaluation reports:

- ◆ Avoid jargon;
- ◆ Use simple, direct language appropriate to the audience;
- ◆ Use examples, anecdotes, illustrations;
- ◆ Use correct spelling, grammar, and punctuation;
- ◆ Avoid cluttering the narrative with reference notes; and,
- ◆ Use language that is interesting, not dull.

## FIGURE 7.5. EVALUATION REPORT OUTLINE

I. Executive summary (usually between 2 and 6 pages in length), the summary should contain a very brief description of the evaluation's purpose and data collection methods used, followed by a presentation of the most important findings, judgments, and recommendations with page references to the full report)

II. Introduction to the report

    A. Purpose of the evaluation (Why was the evaluation conducted? What was the evaluation intended to accomplish? What questions was it intended to answer?)

    B. Audiences for the evaluation report

    C. Limitations of the evaluation and explanation of disclaimers, if any (What conditions or events affected the collection, analysis, or interpretation of information? What is the evaluation? What is it not?)

    D. Overview of report contents

III. Focus of the evaluation

    A. Description of the block schedule program: the rationale for initiating the block schedule, its goals and objectives, its participants, its structure and characteristics, strategies used for implementation of the block schedule, its operating context, and/or resource requirements

    B. Evaluative questions or objectives used to focus the evaluation study

    C. Information used to complete the evaluation

IV. Brief overview of the evaluation plan and procedures (a brief summary of where the information came from and how it was obtained)

V. Presentation of evaluation results

   A. Summary of evaluation findings, using tables, displays, or quotations as appropriate

   B. Interpretation of evaluation findings

VI. Conclusions and recommendations

   A. Criteria and standards used to judge the block schedule

   B. Judgments about the block schedule (strengths and limitations)

   C. Recommendations

VII. Appendices

   A. Description of the evaluation plan/design, instruments, and data analysis and interpretation

   B. Detailed tabulations or analyses of quantitative data, and transcripts or summaries of qualitative data

---

## EVALUATION *DONE* VS. EVALUATION *USED*

Program evaluation is valuable. Scriven (1991) argues that the process of program evaluation is "the process whose duty is the systematic and objective determination of merit, worth, or value. Without such a process, there is no way to distinguish the worthwhile from the worthless" (p. 4). But, just *doing* an evaluation cannot solve the problems of a program. And, when evaluation is done sporadically and unsystematically, the opportunity for continuing self-renewal is lost.

An evaluation does not, in and of itself, effect solutions to problems. An evaluation serves to identify strengths and weaknesses. It is the role of the teachers, staff, and administrators involved in the program to *use* the information obtained to select improvement and staff development targets. It is the role of decision-makers and consumers to *use* evaluation findings to inform the decisions they make about program continuation, revision, or termination.

## SUMMARY

*Don't be a damn ammunition wagon. Be a rifle.*
Carl Rogers

The business of program evaluation is the business of find-ing answers to specific questions aimed at determining the worth or merit of a program. In this chapter, we examined the roles of formal and summative evaluation, the advantages of in-ternal and external evaluators, and key considerations in select-ing an external evaluator, initiating a program evaluation, and committing resources to an evaluation. We also explored key considerations in identifying appropriate audiences for an eval-uation report, developing a program description, developing evaluation questions, determining data collection and analysis strategies, and writing an evaluation report. We presented all of these key considerations because an evaluation means nothing unless it is used for improvement, for staff development selec-tion, and for information-based decision making. An evaluation is more likely to be used if it is feasible and applicable to the school or district's unique needs.

## SUGGESTED READINGS

Canady, R. L., & Rettig, M. D. (1995). *Block scheduling: A catalyst for change in high schools.* Larchmont, NY: Eye on Education.

Hottenstein, D. S. (1998). *Intensive scheduling: Restructuring Amer-ica's secondary schools through time management.* Thousand Oaks, CA: Corwin Press.

Patton, M. Q. (1982). *Practical evaluation.* Thousand Oaks, CA: Sage.

Worthen, B. R., Sanders, J. R., & Fitzpatrick, J. L. (1997). *Program evaluation: Alternative approaches and practical guidelines.* New York: Longman.

# FINAL THOUGHTS

Regardless of whether the block schedule is already in place or the school is moving toward implementing a new schedule, supervisory and staff development practices in the block must change. Without change, the new schedule will not make a difference in learning for stakeholders. With movement toward the block, the principal will be looked to for guidance and assurance from teachers, parents, students, and other members of the school community. It is the principal's knowledge and understanding about the block, his or her ability to involve stakeholders in making critical decisions, and his or her capacity to provide supervision and staff development opportunities that promote growth that will provide guidance for the transition to the block.

Supervision and staff development needs to become embedded as part of each teacher's day. A short-term view of supervisory and staff development initiatives will not endure for the long-term unless the needs of teachers are met at each step of the way in the journey to implement and sustain the block. Like teachers making changes in their classrooms, the principal will need to make changes in providing supervision and staff development that promotes growth and nurtures teachers.

No longer can principals afford to assume that they are solely responsible for *delivering* supervision and staff development. Teachers are the cornerstones of learning in their classrooms. The role of the teacher as learner needs to emerge so that they have an empowered sense of fulfilling their learning needs. The principal's relinquishing of *final authority* over supervision and staff development will inspire confidence and autonomy in teachers.

With a sense of autonomy in identifying needs and tending to them in a more collegial, peer-mediated manner, supervision and staff development must have an elevated position within the structure of the school. Complex to be sure, but the role that teachers need to take in their professional growth is necessary to achieve the primary goal of schools—learning.

Moving to the block can unify a faculty and energize learning. This is the optimism that we wish to communicate to each principal and teacher who reads this book.

# REFERENCES

Acheson, K. A., & Gall, M. D. (1997). *Techniques in the clinical supervision of teachers: Preservice and inservice applications* (4th ed.). White Plains, NY: Longman.

Arnold, G. C. (1995). Teacher dialogues: A constructivist model of staff development. *Journal of Staff Development, 16*(4), 34–38.

Ball, W. H., & Brewer, P. F. (1996). Socratic seminars. In R. L. Canady & M. D. Rettig (Eds.), *Teaching in the block: Strategies for engaging active learners.* (pp. 29–64). Larchmont, NY: Eye on Education.

Barnett, D., McKowen, C., & Bloom, G. (1998). A school without a principal. *Educational Leadership, 55*(7), 48–49.

Bennis, W. (1989). *On becoming a leader.* Reading, MA: Addison-Wesley.

Blase, J., & Blase, J. R. (1994). *Empowering teachers: What successful principals do.* Thousand Oaks, CA: Corwin Press.

Blase, J. R., & Blase, J. (1997). *The fire is back! Principals sharing school governance.* Thousand Oaks, CA: Corwin Press.

Blase, J. R., & Blase, J. (1998). *Handbook of instructional leadership: How really good principals promote teaching and learning.* Thousand Oaks, CA: Corwin Press.

Blumberg, A. (1980). *Supervisors and teachers: A private cold war* (2nd ed.). Berkley, CA: McCutchan.

Brinkerhoff, R. O., Brethower, D. M., Hluchyj, T., & Nowakowski, J. R. (1983). *Program evaluation: A practitioner's guide for trainers and educators.* Boston: Kluwer-Nijhoff.

Brookfield, S. D. (1986). *Understanding and facilitating adult learning.* San Francisco: Jossey-Bass.

Brooks, J. G., & Brooks, M. G. (1993). *In search of understanding: The case for the constructivist classroom.* Alexandria, VA: Association for Supervision and Curriculum.

Brown, B. L. (1997). *Portfolio assessment: Missing link in student evaluation.* Columbus, OH: ERIC Clearinghouse on Adult, Career, and Vocational Education (ERIC Document Reproduction Service No. ED 414 447).

Bruer, J. T. (1998). Brain science, brain fiction. *Educational Leadership, 56*(3), 14–18.

Calabrese, R. L., & Zepeda, S. J. (1997). *The reflective supervisor: A practical guide for educators.* Larchmont, NY: Eye on Education.

Canady, R. L., & Rettig, M. D. (1995). *Block scheduling: A catalyst for change in high schools.* Larchmont, NY: Eye on Education.

Canady, R. L., & Rettig, M. D. (1996). Block scheduling: What is it? Why do it? How do we harness its potential to improve teaching and learning? In R. L. Canady & M. D. Rettig (Eds.), *Teaching in the block: Strategies for engaging active learners.* (pp. 1–27). Larchmont, NY: Eye on Education.

Carroll, J. M. (1990). The Copernican Plan: Restructuring the American high school. *Phi Delta Kappan, 71*(5), 358–365.

Chen, H. (1994). Current trends and future directions in program evaluation. *Evaluation Practice, 15,* 229–238.

Chesley, L. S., Wood, F. H., & Zepeda, S. J. (1997). Induction: Meeting the needs of the alternatively certified teacher. *Journal of Staff Development, 18*(1), 28–32.

Conley, D. T. (1996). *Are you ready to restructure? A guidebook for educators, parents, and community members.* Thousand Oaks, CA: Corwin Press.

Costa, A. L., & Garmston, R. J. (1994). *Cognitive coaching: A foundation for renaissance schools.* Norwood, MA: Christopher-Gordon.

Cousins, J. B., & Leithwood, K. A. (1986). Current empirical research on evaluation utilization. *Review of Educational Research, 56*(3), 331–364.

Covey, S. R., Merrill, A. R., & Merrill, R. R. (1995). *First things first.* New York: Fireside Books.

D'Arcangelo, M. (1998). The brains behind the brain. *Educational Leadership, 56*(3), 20–25.

Darling-Hammond, L. (1995). Restructuring schools for student success. *Daedalus, 124*(4), 153–156.

Dewey, J. W. (1938). *Education and experience.* New York: Collier MacMillan.

English, F. (1984). Curriculum mapping and management. In B. D. Sattes (Ed.), *Promoting school excellence through the application of effective schools research: Summary and proceedings of a 1984 regional exchange workshop* (ERIC Document Reproduction Services No. ED 251 972).

Fullan, M. (1993). *Change forces: Probing the depths of educational reform.* Bristol, PA: Falmer Press.

Gardner, H. (1993). *Frames of mind: The theory of multiple intelligences.* New York: Basic Books.

Garman, N. B. (1982). The clinical approach to supervision. In T. J. Sergiovanni (Ed.), *Supervision of teaching.* Alexandria, VA: Association for Supervision and Curriculum.

Gilkey, S. N., & Hunt, C. H. (1998). *Teaching mathematics in the block.* Larchmont, NY: Eye on Education.

Glanz, J. (1998). *Action research: An educational leader's guide to school improvement.* Norwood, MA: Christopher-Gordon.

Glickman, C. D., Gordon, S. P., & Ross-Gordon, J. M. (1998). *Supervision of instruction: A developmental approach* (4th ed.). Boston: Allyn & Bacon.

Gordon, S. P. (1999). Ready? How effective schools know it's time to take the plunge. *Journal of Staff Development, 20*(1), 48–53.

Guba, E. G., & Lincoln, Y. S. (1981). *Effective evaluation.* San Francisco: Jossey-Bass.

Hirsh, S., & Ponder, G. (1991). New plots, new heroes in staff development. *Educational Leadership, 49*(3), 43–48.

Hong, L. K. (1996). *Surviving school reform: A year in the life of one school.* New York: Teachers College Press.

Hord, S., & Cowan, D. (1999). Creating learning communities. *Journal of Staff Development, 20*(2), 44–45.

Hottenstein, D. S. (1998). *Intensive scheduling: Restructuring America's secondary schools through time management.* Thousand Oaks, CA: Corwin Press.

Howey, K. R., & Vaughn, J. C. (1983). Current patterns of staff development. In G. A. Griffin (Ed.), *Staff development, Eighty-second Yearbook of the National Society for the Study of Education.* (pp. 228–250). Chicago: The University of Chicago Press.

Huntress, J., & Jones, L. (1999). *Reflective process tools.* Training Materials Developed for the Putnam City Principal Preparation Cohort in conjunction with the University of Oklahoma, Norman, OK.

Jensen, E. (1998). *Teaching with the brain in mind.* Alexandria, VA: Association for Supervision and Curriculum Development.

Johnson, D. W., & Johnson, R. T. (1990). Social skills for successful group work. *Educational Leadership, 47*(4), 29–33.

Johnson, D. W., & Johnson, R. T. (1994). Learning together. In S. Sharan (Ed.), *Handbook of cooperative learning methods.* (pp. 51–65). Westport, CT: Greenwood Press.

Johnson, D. W., Johnson, R. T., & Smith, K. (1991). *Active learning: Cooperation in the college classroom.* Edina, MN: Interaction Book Company.

Joint Committee on Standards for Educational Evaluation. (1994). *The program evaluation standards* (2nd ed.). Thousand Oaks, CA: Sage.

Joyce, B. R., & Showers, B. (1982). The coaching of teaching. *Educational Leadership, 40*(1), 4–8.

Joyce, B. R., & Weil, M. (1996). *Models of Teaching* (5th ed.). Boston: Allyn & Bacon.

Kagan, S. (1992). *Cooperative learning.* San Juan Capistrano, CA: Resources for Teachers.

Kagan, S. (1995). Group grades miss the mark. *Educational Leadership, 52*(8), 68–71.

Klecker, B. J., & Loadman, W. E. (1998). Defining and measuring the dimensions of teacher empowerment in restructuring public schools. *Education, 118*(3), 358–371.

Lucas, S., Brown, G. C., & Markus, F. W. (1991). Principal's perceptions of site-based management and teacher empowerment. *NASSP Bulletin, 75*(537), 56–62.

Lunenburg, F. C. (1995). *The principalship: Concepts and applications.* Englewood Cliffs, NJ: Merrill.

Lybbert, B. (1998). *Transforming learning with block scheduling: A guide for principals.* Thousand Oaks, CA: Corwin Press.

Makibbin, S., & Sprague, M. (1991). *Study groups: Conduit for reform.* St. Louis, MO: National Staff Development Council (ERIC Document Reproduction Service No. ED 370 893).

Marsh, D., & Daro, P. (1999). Rethinking curriculum and instruction in the new American high school. In D. Marsh and J.B. Codding (Eds.), *The new American high school* (pp. 62–88). Thousand Oaks, CA: Corwin Press.

Marshall, C. (1992). *The assistant principal: Leadership choices and challenges.* Thousand Oaks, CA: Corwin Press.

Marshak, D. (1997). *Action research on block scheduling.* Larchmont, NY: Eye on Education.

McBride, M., & Skau, K.G. (1995). Trust, empowerment, and reflection: Essentials of supervision. *Journal of Curriculum and Supervision, 10*(3), 262–277.

McCall, J. (1997). *The principal as steward.* Larchmont, NY: Eye on Education.

McGreal, T. (1983). *Effective Teacher Evaluation.* Alexandria, VA: Association for Curriculum and Supervision.

McQuarrie, F. O., & Wood, F. H. (1991). Supervision, staff development, and evaluation connections. *Theory Into Practice, 30*(2), 91–96.

Murphy, S. M. (1997). Designing portfolio assessment: Programs to enhance learning. *The Clearing House, 71*(2), 81–84.

North Carolina State Department of Public Instruction (1997). *Foreign languages on the block.* Raleigh, NC: Department of Public Instruction (ERIC Document Reproduction Service No. ED 403 742).

O'Neil, J. (1998). Constructivism—Wanted: Deep understanding. In J. O'Neil & S. Willis (Eds.), *Transforming classroom prac-*

*tice* (pp. 49–70). Alexandria, VA: Association for Supervision and Curriculum Development.

Orlich, D.C., Harder, R.J., Callahan, R.C., Kauchak, D.P., & Gibson, H.W. (1994). *Teaching strategies: A guide to better instruction* (4th ed.). Lexington, MA: D.C. Heath.

Pajak, E. (1993). *Approaches to clinical supervision: Alternatives for improving instruction.* Norwood, MA: Christopher-Gordon.

Pascarelli, J. T., & Ponticell,J.A. (1994). Trust-blocking responses. Training Materials Developed for Co-Teaching. Chicago, IL.

Pasternack, B. A., & Viscio, A. J. (1998). *The centerless corporation: A new model for transforming your organization for growth and prosperity.* New York: Simon & Schuster.

Ponticell, J. A. (1995). Promoting teaching professionalism through collegiality. *Journal of Staff Development, 16*(3), 13–18.

Queen, J. A., & Isenhour, K. G. (1998). *The 4 x 4 block schedule.* Larchmont, NY: Eye on Education.

Rogers, C. R. (1961). *On becoming a person.* Boston: Houghton-Mifflin.

Sanders, J. R. (1979). The technology and art of evaluation. A review of seven evaluation primers. *Evaluation News, 12,* 2–7.

Sarason, S. B. (1992). *The predictable failure of educational reform: Can we change course before it's too late?* San Francisco: Jossey-Bass.

Sarason, S. B. (1997). *How schools might be governed and why.* New York: Teachers College Press.

Scriven, M. (1967). The methodology of evaluation. In R. E. Stake (Ed.), *Curriculum evaluation.* (American Educational Research Association Monograph Series on Evaluation, No. 1, pp. 39–83). Chicago, IL: Rand McNally.

Scriven, M. (1991). *Evaluation thesaurus* (4th ed.). Newbury Park, CA: Sage.

Senge, P. M. (1990). *The fifth discipline: The art and practice of the learning organization.* New York: Currency Doubleday.

Sergiovanni, T. J. (1992). *Moral leadership: Getting to the heart of school improvement.* San Francisco: Jossey-Bass.

Sergiovanni, T. J. (1996). *Leadership for the schoolhouse: How is it different? Why is it important?* San Francisco: Jossey-Bass.

Sergiovanni, T. J., & Starratt, R. J. (1998). *Supervision: A redefinition* (6th ed.). Boston: McGraw-Hill.

Sharan, S., & Sharan, Y. (1976). *Small-group teaching.* Englewood Cliffs, NJ: Educational Technology Publications.

Shen, J. (1998). Do teachers feel empowered? *Educational Leadership, 55*(7), 35–36.

Showers, B. (1985). Teachers coaching teachers. *Educational Leadership, 42*(7), 43–48.

Siens, C.M., & Ebmeir, H. (1996). Developmental supervision and the reflective thinking of teachers. *Journal of Curriculum and Supervision, 11*(4), 299–319.

Sparks, D., & Hirsh, S. (1997). *A new vision for staff development.* Oxford, OH: National Staff Development Council.

Starratt, R. J. (1995). *Leaders with vision: The quest for school renewal.* Thousand Oaks, CA: Corwin Press.

Strebe, J. D. (1996). The collaborative classroom. In R. L. Canady & M. D. Rettig (Eds.), *Teaching in the block: Strategies for engaging active learners.* (pp. 65–106). Larchmont, NY: Eye on Education.

Suchman, J. R. (1962). *The elementary school training program in scientific inquiry* (Report No. NDEA-VIIA-216). Urbana, IL: University of Illinois (ERIC Document Reproduction Service No. ED 003 530).

Tanner, B., Canady, R. L., & Rettig, M. D. (1995). Scheduling time to maximize staff development opportunities. *Journal of Staff Development, 16*(4), 14–19.

Walker, D. E. (1998). *Strategies for teaching differently: On the block or not.* Thousand Oaks, CA: Corwin Press.

Winebrenner, S. (1992). *Teaching gifted kids in the regular classroom: Strategies and techniques every teacher can use to meet the academic needs of the gifted and talented.* Minneapolis, MN: Free Spirit Publishing.

Wolfe, P., & Brandt, R. (1998). What do we know from brain research? *Educational Leadership, 56*(3), 8–13.

Wood, F. H., & Killian, J. (1998). Job-embedded learning makes the difference in school improvement. *Journal of Staff Development, 19*(1), 52–54.

Wood, F. H., Killian, J., McQuarrie, F. M., & Thompson, S. (1993). *How to organize a school-based staff development program.* Alexandria, VA: Association for Supervision and Curriculum Development.

Worthen, B. R., & Sanders, J. R. (1987). *Educational evaluation: Alternative approaches and practical guidelines.* New York: Longman.

Worthen, B. R., Sanders, J. R., & Fitzpatrick, J. L. (1997). *Program evaluation: Alternative approaches and practical guidelines.* New York: Longman.

Wyatt, L. D. (1996). More time, more training: What staff development do teachers need for effective instruction in block scheduling? *The School Administrator, 58*(8), 16–18.

Zepeda, S. J. (1994, February). *Conflicts in supervisory practices: A preliminary exploration.* Paper presented at the Annual Meeting of the Association of Teacher Educators, Detroit, MI.

Zepeda, S. J. (1995). How to ensure positive responses in classroom observations. *Tips for Principals: National Association of Secondary School Principals.* Reston, VA: National Association of Secondary School Principals.

Zepeda, S. J. (1999a). *Staff development: Practices that promote leadership in learning communities.* Larchmont, NY: Eye on Education.

Zepeda, S. J. (1999b). Arrange time into blocks. *Journal of Staff Development, 20*(2), 26–30.

Zepeda, S. J., & Ponticell, J. A. (1995). The supervisory continuum: A developmental approach. *NASSP Practitioner, 22*(1), 1–4.

# INDEX OF NAMES

# INDEX BY TOPIC

# H

# I

**J, K**

**L**

**R**